ON CALL

The Work of a Telephone Helpline for Child Abusers

AUP Titles of Related Interest

CHILDREN NEED GROUPS
W R Silveira and Gill Trafford

MARITAL THERAPY: AN INSIDE VIEW
Christopher Clulow

TO HAVE AND TO HOLD
Christopher Clulow

A CELEBRATION OF MARRIAGE?
Scotland 1931-81: implications for marital counselling and therapy
J D Haldane

ON CALL

The Work of a Telephone Helpline for Child Abusers

WARREN COLMAN

ABERDEEN UNIVERSITY PRESS

First published 1989
Aberdeen University Press
A member of the Pergamon Group

British Library Cataloguing in Publication Data

Colman, Warren
On call : the work of a telephone helpline for child abusers.
1. Great Britian. Children. Abuse by parents.
Prevention. Prevention of child abuse by parents.
Role of telephone services
I. Title
362.7′044

ISBN 0–08–037958–3

Typeset, printed and bound in Great Britain by
BPCC Hazell Books Ltd
Member of BPCC Ltd
Aylesbury, Bucks, England

Contents

Acknowledgements

When Janet Mattinson, then Chairman of TIMS, and Evelyn Cleavely, Co-ordinator of Training, asked me to join with Evelyn in offering a series of training workshops for the volunteers of a telephone helpline for abusing parents I was still serving my apprenticeship at TIMS and I would now like to thank them both for giving me the opportunity to participate in the work with Parents Anonymous, on which this monograph is based. My especial appreciation is due to Evelyn Cleavely, my co-worker throughout the project. Although the responsibility for the actual writing rests with me, many of the ideas expressed here are hers and many more were developed with the help of her unusually sympathetic encouragement. I learned a great deal from working alongside her and would like to say how much I continue to value her clinical wisdom.

All my TIMS colleagues have been supportive of this work and have contributed their thoughts and reactions but I am particularly grateful to Christopher Clulow to whose greater experience of writing I turned when I felt I was in danger of drowning in this, my first substantial writing project, and who unfailingly baled me out. I would also like to express my appreciation of all the volunteers of Parents Anonymous who gave up their own time to come to the workshops in addition to their 'on call' work for the helpline itself and, for many, the administrative work of running the organisation. In the workshops they gave generously of themselves and this monograph, which is essentially a record of the insights that emerged from those workshops, would not have been possible without their commitment and enthusiasm. I would like to thank them, too, for their permission to use case material from their work with callers to the helpline. In a number of places in the text I refer both implicitly and explicitly to how much Evelyn Cleavely and I valued the work that Parents Anonymous does but it also seems appropriate to record that appreciation here.

Introduction

Telephone helplines are a relatively new phenomenon in the world of the helping professions. Apart from the Samaritans, who opened for business in 1953, most have grown up in the last ten years or so. They represent a spontaneous response to specific areas of felt need, often run on a shoe-string basis by enthusiastic volunteers with an aura of the self-help group about them. Even Childline, with its much higher profile, larger size and budget than any other helpline except the Samaritans shares with them the spontaneous response to a matter of public concern and the fact that it is predominantly staffed by volunteers. In other words, telephone helplines exist outside the usual network of professional services.

From 1984 to 1986 my colleague Evelyn Cleavely and I, both marital psychotherapists of the then Institute of Marital Studies (now Tavistock Institute of Marital Studies), ran a series of training workshops for the volunteer workers of Parents Anonymous (London), a telephone helpline for parents under stress, particularly those at risk of abusing their children. In the course of these workshops we came to have a deep respect for the courage and dedication with which these comparatively untrained, but not unskilled, volunteers dealt with situations of acute danger and distress via the fragile link of telecommunication. This was a field that was as new to us as we were new to them and it is the aim of this monograph to share the insights that emerged from this unusual 'marriage'. We believe that these insights will have relevance not only for Parents Anonymous but for telephone helplines generally since many of the issues about the helping relationship which arose in the course of the workshops, if not unique to telephone work, were strongly slanted by that particular helping context

The monograph is also concerned with the content of the work, namely child abuse, as well as the arena of the telephone helpline in which it was presented. Telephone helplines exist as alternatives or auxiliaries to the professional network of services and therefore have a different clientele from the professionals or at least receive a different aspect of their problems. There is probably no such thing as a 'solution' to a problem like child abuse but the response to telephone helplines set up to tackle it (whether those attempting to reach the potential perpetrators as with Parents Anonymous or the victims as with Childline) shows that existing professional services are certainly not perceived as having all the available answers.

Those involved in this difficult and complex field will no doubt hear much that is familiar to them in the calls made to Parents Anonymous but they also provide a glimpse into the stressful life of many families from a vantage point very different from that of the social worker, paediatrician or health visitor. Not least, many of these calls were made at moments of acute crisis by people who did *not* want to contact the statutory services, and wanted to remain anonymous. There is much to be learned here about the stresses that precipitate child abuse and the anxieties that inhibit abusers from seeking appropriate help. However, there is also the further question of whether such help would, in any case, be available. For what are, no doubt, good reasons, social workers and others have become intensely preoccupied in recent years with situations which require urgent action, often the removal of children from their parents. As well as taking up an increasing amount of their time so that preventative and ameliorative work has inevitably suffered, the public perception of their statutory role has made many potential clients afraid to approach social workers for fear of losing their children. Parents Anonymous has felt the effects of all this in an increased demand for their services and a greater range and complexity of 'serious' calls. This highlights the challenge of what help can be provided by a telephone helpline. The view presented here is that their main role is *the provision of a listening ear* but the value of listening itself provides, in turn, a challenge to professionals who may, especially nowadays, find themselves 'too busy' to listen.

Thirdly, the relationship between volunteers and professionals is addressed. Most of the literature on this subject appears to be from the professional point of view—e.g. how to train and deploy volunteers in professional contexts. In this study the reverse applies: professionals are seen from the volunteer's point of view. The PA volunteers' attitude to professionals revealed much about the fantasies and anxieties stemming from their own position but it also threw light on how professionals are seen by *outsiders*—clients as much as volunteers. The volunteers were often much closer to their callers' world than the professionals, with all the attendant strengths and weaknesses that this implies. A grass roots organisation like Parents Anonymous is a model example of Community Care in practice. It is both a spontaneous response by the community for the community but is also public service organisation. It straddles these two worlds whose goals do not always dovetail as well as they might and at its best can mediate between them. There is no question of Parents Anonymous being able to supplant statutory services but nor is it likely that a statutory service can ever fulfil the role of an anonymous telephone helpline. Volunteers and professionals need each other.

Fourthly, it is to be hoped that this account of their work will bring Parents Anonymous to wider public notice. We are partisan in this respect. We were often astonished at the difficulties the volunteers faced in their work and admiring of their willingness to go on giving their time and effort to it. We came to believe that Parents Anonymous has a useful and, if properly defined, a unique role to play in helping parents in trouble. This monograph sets out to describe that role through an exploration of how we arrived at a more precise definition of it in the course of the workshops.

This is very much a case study. There are many more telephone helplines than PA; indeed Parents Anonymous, London is only one of many such groups spread across the country under the umbrella of OPUS—the Organisation for Parents Under Stress (recently renamed Parentline). Not everything that is true for PA, London will be true for these other groups but my aim has been to point up issues of general relevance in the particular 'case' rather than getting lost in a mass of individual details for their own sake.

The workshops and their subsequent writing-up were undertaken under the aegis of the Tavistock Institute of Marital Studies, and were informed by the psychoanalytically based theory of interaction that has characterised other TIMS projects and publications. The TIMS approach can be described as an application of an application—i.e. psychoanalysis as applied to the field of marital interaction is further applied to a range of settings where client and worker meet outside the privileged arrangements of the psychotherapeutic situation. The common denominator is the attempt to understand marital, family and client/worker interaction in terms which, while psychoanalytic in origin, are approachable by those who are not schooled in that particular theoretical framework. Nevertheless the phenomena which the theory enables us to address are complex and it is not possible to write about theory without making demands on the reader's understanding. Where technical terms are used I have given an explanation of them but I have not tried to exclude them altogether because I believe them to provide useful ways of thinking about the material. I hope I have not used 'jargon', however since, in my view, technical terms only degenerate into jargon when they are used for their own sake as a substitute for stating clearly the writer's meaning.

The work has also found its own length—considerably more than a journal article but rather less than a full length book—hence, a monograph. It begins with a description of Parents Anonymous and of the training project that TIMS devised with them at their request. As this was an unusual venture for us we were interested in there being a research component from the outset. All of the first series of workshops were tape-recorded although, apart from providing some direct quotations, these proved to be more of a hindrance than a help and, in the subsequent workshops, we relied on our own detailed notes.

The second chapter describes the various different kinds of calls received by Parents Anonymous and includes a discussion of the particular difficulties raised by incest callers, i.e. sexual abusers. These difficulties are twofold: the stress on the worker due to the powerful emotions which the subject of incest arouses, and the peculiar blurring of the usual distinctions between fantasy and reality which seems to occur whenever incest is involved.

In Chapters 3 and 4 the situation of volunteers working in the stressful field of child abuse with little protection or support is compared and contrasted with that of professional carers, from the point of view of both worker and client.

Chapter 3 looks at the various reasons why people may choose to contact a telephone helpline rather than seeking help through some other agency, and explores the role that helplines can play in the overall network of services. It is here that the value of the worker being able to listen to the caller's distress and tune in to their particular anxieties is emphasised.

This leads on in Chapter 4 to a discussion of the complexities of the relationship between workers and callers. Although the psychoanalytic theory of transference and counter-transference has already been referred to, this chapter draws most explicitly on psychoanalytic thinking, making use of concepts such as projective identification, unconscious fantasy* and primitive defences such as omnipotence.

In the last two chapters an attempt is made to make a broader assessment of our work with Parents Anonymous. The impact of the training on the workshop members and the organisation as a whole is discussed in Chapter 5, focusing on the theme of appropriate boundary setting. Chapter 6 is a brief discussion of the wider social situation to which telephone helplines are a response and to which they contribute.

*I have not followed the usual psychoanalytic convention of spelling fantasy with a 'ph' when it refers to unconscious mental processes as it is often impossible to distinguish clearly between the two and the distinction then becomes more confusing than clarifying.

CHAPTER ONE

The Project

Parents Anonymous, London (PA)

Parents Anonymous, London is one of a number of similar groups in this country affiliated to OPUS, the Organisation for Parents Under Stress. Most of these groups offer a telephone helpline, some also offer befriending, drop-in centres and practical help, e.g. crèches. In the USA where the idea of Parents Anonymous started in the 1970s there are now over 500 such groups.

The stated aim of OPUS is to 'break the cycle of child abuse'. One of their leaflets outlines their policy thus: 'OPUS believes that isolation is one of the main stresses leading to child abuse. By encouraging parents to come together, to help each other grow and develop as parents and to be available to other parents under stress, OPUS volunteers believe that stress can be alleviated'.

This suggests that OPUS groups offer a form of self-help. PA, London was in fact started by a battering parent but in the words of their own information leaflet 'the rest of the organisation's committee are mainly motivated by the feeling of "there but for the grace of God go I".' In other words, although all volunteers are parents and the group is therefore run by parents for parents, they are not usually abusers themselves. The ethos is rather that, as fellow parents, they are in a position to understand the stresses which lead *some* parents to abuse their children and that this shared understanding has a positive role to play in the prevention of child abuse. For PA, London, at any rate, the work of offering the telephone helpline service has become primary and the more self-help-like aspects of 'coming together to grow as parents' have faded into the background. It may be that this is due to the sheer size of a group attempting to cover the whole of London and also the consequent demands made on it by its potential clientele.

PA, London began in 1976 and by 1983 there were between fifty and sixty volunteers, almost all women. This number has remained fairly steady ever since. Every volunteer is provided with a basic training consisting of six group sessions including discussion by 'experts', role-play, films about child abuse etc. Some selection occurs through these sessions but it is mainly self-selection—i.e. people deciding for themselves that it is not for them.

After the basic training volunteers go onto a rota for 'on-call' duties—usually one night every three weeks. All the calls are received in the workers' own homes. There is a central telephone number with an ansaphone which gives the telephone number of the worker on call at that time.

There is an Organiser and a Committee which nominally runs PA but our impression was of a very loose organisation with little structure and supervision of work. Area-based leaderless support groups meet monthly and are often concerned more with admin and business matters than looking directly at the work. There is also a team of professional 'back-ups' who are available for consultation—mainly social workers, plus a couple of doctors, a psychologist/nurse and a barrister.

We discovered that the back-ups were very much under-used, ironically because the workers felt unable to share their difficulties with the 'anonymous' back-up and felt the need for a more personal face-to-face contact with them. They also had an image of the professional back-ups as too busy, too 'important' and not really interested in them. These ambivalent feelings about the back-ups—wanting their help but fearing and feeling critical of them—were characteristic of their feelings towards the professional network of services in general.

Linking up with the Tavistock Institute of Marital Studies (TIMS)

The TIMS was approached by a volunteer member of Parents Anonymous in May 1983. She wrote asking if we could provide some training for the volunteers who were concerned about their capacity to handle the increasing range and complexity of calls they were receiving, particularly those involving incest.

This was an unusual request for TIMS which usually operates as a centre for advanced study offering training at a post-qualifying level. The TIMS staff are themselves all highly trained professionals, mainly in the fields of social work and psychotherapy—a very different world from that of the volunteer. Nevertheless, the request from PA offered us an innovative opportunity to test our belief in the applicability of our basic approach to a variety of other settings.

Our aim was to apply our understanding of interaction to the specific needs of their situation without attempting to turn them into quasi-professionals. We were clear from the outset that, whether actually self-help or not, the nature of PA as an organisation run by ordinary parents for ordinary parents was essential to its role and that if our intervention were to change the nature of that organisation it would only create a vacuum which another PA would have to fill. In the event, this initial aim proved to be a difficult tightrope to walk in view of the demands being made on the volunteers by some callers who were anything but ordinary parents. In retrospect, it was apparent that the request for training itself arose in the context of the organisation's move away from its self-help beginnings.

The most usual method of TIMS training is 1½ hour workshops where cases are presented and discussed. The workshop model is well suited to conveying the method of work which we teach, since the manner of working in the workshop—by reflecting on and discussing 'live' material—is closely analogous to the way we actually work with our clients. These case-discussion groups are truly workshops in that they provide an opportunity to try out and practise ideas which can then be taken back into the work and tested out. In addition the workshop model provides a flexible tool for applying our concepts and methods to a wide range of different settings since it encourages workers to bring *their own work* to us with which we can then engage together. The workshop itself thus provides the bridge between the worker's world and our world. The process of application begins in the creative exchange between two different worlds.

One might ask why an Institute of Marital Studies should have something to offer a group of workers whose main concern is child abuse? Apart from the obvious fact that in many situations where parents are under stress there is also a marriage under stress, we have a more fundamental reason for believing in the relevance of what we have learned from the study of marriages to the wider field of family and also client/worker interaction. We regard marriage as a paradigmatic model of two person interaction since it is the arena par excellence where internal conflicts arising from formative childhood relationships are expressed and, if all goes well, can be worked out. The study of marital interaction thus provides a unique opportunity to understand processes of interaction which occur in all intimate relationships (including the helping relationship). The insights gleaned can then be applied to the task of managing a helping relationship to the best advantage of the client.

In our training workshops we place considerable emphasis on working with the feelings evoked in the workers by their clients and also the process whereby aspects of the client/worker interaction are reflected in the experience and behaviour of the workshop participants (Mattinson

1975). The tendency for aspects of the clients' inner world to 'get into' the workers is now well known in psychoanalysis as an important aspect of the 'counter-transference'—i.e. the response that is elicited in the therapist by the client's transference of feelings and expectations from other, usually past, arenas of his or her life. Thus, instead of trying to screen out their feelings as extraneous to the client's problem, therapists now recognise that their feeling response may be a powerful source of information about the client's difficulties and strive to subject their own responses to as detailed a scrutiny as those of the client. We regarded it as an interesting and valuable challenge to see whether such sophisticated concepts as counter-transference could be grasped by the largely untrained and unsophisticated volunteers of PA.

The training format we eventually offered consisted of weekly 1½ hour workshops to be held in two blocks of eight weeks each. The workshops were to be co-led by Evelyn Cleavely and Warren Colman. In the description circulated to all PA members we described our aims as follows

> to give support to workers and to enable them to become more effective in dealing with calls by providing opportunities 1) to explore in detail what was actually said by the caller and the helper and whether the helper said what he/she would like to have said and 2) to attempt to make sense of the feelings and responses evoked.

It will be seen that in this description we were providing essentially the same model as used for our usual post-qualifying training but already beginning the task of communicating our approach in language tailored to meet the needs of this particular group of potential 'trainees'.

Description of the Project

One week before the workshops were due to start we heard that there had been a disappointing response from the members and the whole project might have to be called off. It is indicative of the loose organisation in PA that the impetus for the workshops had come from an individual member (i.e. not from the organiser or the Committee) and she had taken it upon herself to promote the course to the other members. It now looked as though this individual worker's enthusiasm for further training was not shared by her colleagues although there was some indication that the lack of enthusiasm was for PA itself. With hindsight we would see the sense of confusion and ambivalence as symptomatic of an organisation exposed to considerable pressure and unsure of its direction.

As it turned out, the workshop began with nine PA workers, plus one of the social worker back-ups who had expressed an interest. To our surprise, considering the uncertainty immediately prior to the workshop's beginning, the members maintained a high level of commitment to the group, with most (though not all!) attending regularly and on time. This is the more impressive when one takes into account that this was a group of volunteers, with families of their own, giving up an evening a week (in addition to their 'on-call' time) to turn out often on cold winter nights and, for many, having to travel half way across London to get to us.

As the group developed its own life and the members became convinced of the value of what we had to offer, they began to think about the group's relation to PA as a whole. They felt that a divide was opening up between them and the rest of the organisation. PA members not in the group continued to express very ambivalent feelings about the workshop, some feeling it was not relevant or appropriate to PA, some threatened by it, some envious, some openly acknowledging that they felt they were 'missing out'. This range of feelings is again indicative of the turbulence within PA as to its own nature. Was it an inspirational self-help group, its offer of help guaranteed—and also limited—by its members status as 'ordinary parents' or did the demands made on it by callers require it to be more than that—to be able to offer, at the least, a specialised skill of 'listening' or even 'counselling' and for its members to possess some specialised knowledge, e.g. of incest? If the latter argument was accepted was there then a danger of it becoming 'professionalised' out of its role, bearing in mind the prevailing ethos of 'professionals' as 'too busy' and 'too important' to listen to their troubles?

This dilemma ran right through our involvement with PA and is a major theme of this monograph. However, the workshop itself proved to be a major factor influencing the climate of debate within the organisation. In June 1985, a year after the first workshop had ended, we were approached with a request to run a second series of workshops. This we agreed to do offering twenty sessions instead of sixteen. Members were also asked to contribute £20 each.

By this time the climate of opinion had clearly changed in PA and the response to the offered workshop was such that we were asked to run two groups instead of one. To keep costs down and because we were more experienced with PA's work we offered to run each workshop with single leadership, with Evelyn Cleavely taking one group of ten including two back-ups and four members of the first workshop coming back for more, and Warren Colman taking a second group of nine new members, also including two back-ups.

In this second series the back-ups had a slightly more ambiguous role. One of the results of the first workshop had been to increase the workers' awareness of the need to make greater use of their back-ups and, in fact, it turned out that the back-ups themselves complained of being under-used. In this second series of workshops we were keen to begin to pass the torch of teaching, support and supervision from ourselves to those within the organisation itself. In our external training projects it is a long established tradition in the TIMS to co-lead with a member of the host agency. This is, of course, a further means of creating a bridge between our own knowledge base and its application to a different setting. We had hoped to co-lead the second series with the back-up social worker who had attended the first series but she was unfortunately unable to join us due to ill-health. We did not feel it would be possible to co-lead with back-ups who did not already know something of our world but nevertheless saw their presence in the group as fostering their potential leadership role in PA as a whole. The fact that the back-ups were deliberately circulated with details of the workshop and that four of them offered to come, again points up the shift in attitudes that was already taking place in PA about the relationship between professionals and volunteers.

We also noticed a change of culture between the members of the two sets of workshops. It was as though all the members, not just the four people in Evelyn Cleavely's group, had attended the previous workshops. There was greater sophistication and more interest in developing counselling skills and acquiring 'expert' knowledge. Several members had related experience, e.g. one worked for MIND, one had been a Samaritan, one was on a part-time counselling course and another went into a full-time counselling course after the workshop ended.

We do not know how 'typical' of PA workers our members were, but at twenty-two out of a total of fifty to sixty they numbered over one third of the total membership. Socially they were a heterogeneous group, some working class, some middle class. Four of the twenty-two were teachers and one was a Home Help Organiser. None of the others were professionals and in fact the teachers shared the prevailing ambivalent attitude towards professionals in the helping professions.

Their length of involvement with PA ranged from one year to seven years, i.e. from its inception. The average in both workshops was three years although in the second series there was a greater range, i.e. more new members and also more with five years' plus experience. The length of experience, though, was no particular guide to the level of sophistication of individual members and although those who had additional counselling experience were inevitably amongst the more sophisticated, some of the best work was done by people who had no formal training or experience. Some people might say that these women were simply ordinary mothers with plenty of common sense but the reality is that this kind of sense is far from common.

CHAPTER TWO

The Calls

The discussion in this chapter is, of course, based on a pre-selected sample of PA calls. We only know about those calls presented at the Workshop and it is not possible to say with any certainty how far they reflected all the calls received. Nevertheless, some calls were presented as being 'typical' and others as problematic or downright extraordinary. The calls that were least likely to be presented to the group were those which could be dealt with purely by giving practical information. Such information would usually consist of referral to another agency. Other forms of ostensibly practical information, e.g. about child care, were usually inseparable from issues to do with the emotional climate of the parent/child relationship.

Out of a total of forty-eight workshops (a further three were spent on reviewing the course and five were not recorded) we heard about 123 calls. Of these, twenty-three were mentioned in passing or in relation to other calls being discussed in more detail (e.g. a batch of calls from an evening's work would be described and one or two then chosen to work on). In one or two of the early workshops of the first series we were deluged by anecdotal accounts of 'strange calls we have had at some time or other' and these sessions account for fifteen of the twenty-three 'No detail' calls. These sessions, though, served a useful purpose in enabling workers to offload a lot of the bizarre, baffling and disturbing calls to which they had been subjected and enabling us to get an impression of the range of calls received by PA. Pretty soon, however, the group settled down to looking in some detail at an average of two or three calls each session.

Most calls were one-off contacts and, for the workers, this was one of the most frustrating aspects of the work. They had only one shot at helping the caller and often never knew how effective they had been or indeed whether they had helped at all. Apart from the enormous anxiety this left them with it also made it very difficult for them to assess their methods of work or to have any criteria for knowing whether they should alter their approach and, if so, how?

A few callers, however, struck up long-term relationships with individual workers. Ironically, these were not necessarily the most successful—in the course of both series of workshops we needed to help workers disentangle themselves from unproductive and debilitating collusions with callers whom they could not actually help (some of these calls are considered in more detail below).

PA was originally set up to offer help in the specific area of Child Abuse: the original poster carried the message 'Don't hurt your Child—Call us!' By the time we came to work with them, however, they had extended their official catchment group to the more general 'Parents Under Stress'. The new poster says—'Desperate, Worried, Under Stress, Family Problems. Don't worry alone. Instead Ring us . . .' and a leaflet specifies that a service is available to 'any parent who may have problems with their babies, toddlers and older children'. The calls brought to the group bore out this wider focus, as the following table shows.

TABLE OF CALLS

	1st Series		2nd Series		Total		*Female Callers* (Overall total = 62%)	*Male Callers* (Overall total = 38%)
Focus of Problem								
Child Abuse	25%	(13)	21%	(15)	23%	(28)	89%	11%
Child Care	17%	(9)	10%	(7)	13%	(16)	94%	6%
Teenagers (+ Adult Children)	23%	(12)	15%	(11)	19%	(23)	67%	33%
Incest	13%	(6)	21%	(15)	18%	(22)	18%	82%
Incest Victims	6%	(3)	3%	(2)	4%	(5)	60%	40%
Personal	6%	(3)	7%	(5)	6%	(8)	62%	38%
Family/Marital	4%	(2)	6%	(4)	5%	(6)	67%	33%
Hoax/Fantasy	–		14%	(10)	8%	(10)	50%	50%
Sex Calls	6%	(3)	3%	(2)	4%	(5)	–	100%
	100%	(52)	100%	(71)	100%	(123)		

Notes on the Table of Calls

1) Hoax/Fantasy Calls. In the first series there were eight calls thought to be hoaxes, all concerning sex. But the 'hoax' element did not emerge as the *focus* of the problem presented. In the second series some of the 'hoax' calls were so elaborate and bizarre that they served to sensitise the group to this issue as a specific—and often intensely difficult—problem.

   If one adds these eight 'disguised' hoax calls, plus three similarly undesignated calls from the second series the total for these calls looks quite different—i.e. 17% (21). If it were possible to quantify the time and energy spent on them, both actually on the phone and in the group, the figure would be much greater.

2) Despite the range of calls and the frequent sense that PA was being inundated with many inappropriate calls, these were only a very small number in which a child/parent relation did not figure at all (6–7% calls). In other words 94% of callers

presented either as parents or as abused children (or both!) What was much harder to distinguish was whether the being a parent was merely a ticket of entry or whether, conversely, many problems presented as primarily personal or family/marital, for example, concealed an undisclosed child abuse element. There were many occasions when the question 'Why PA?' proved very revealing and many more when it might have done had it been asked.

3) Incest Calls. The few women callers were not themselves abusers but were calling about sexual abuse of which their husbands, and in one case, son, were suspected. However, the two male victims claimed to have been seduced by female relatives (step-mother, aunt). There was no ostensible reason to doubt their stories.

Child Care and Child Abuse Calls

The distinction between a Child Care call and a Child Abuse call was often a very difficult one to make. The vast majority of the abuse callers were in a state of fear, rage and panic—at the end of their tether. Some had just hit a child, others feared they might do so. In other cases, however, the predominant feeling was of desperation and not being able to cope, often with a crying baby or less often a toddler having a tantrum. Although there is always the *possibility* of abuse in such cases, it seemed a less pressing one—and was not presented as such. These kind of calls have therefore been classified as Child Care calls. Notably less of these calls were presented in the second series and there are three possible reasons for this. Some workers said that the number of serious and dramatic calls—i.e. the abuse calls requiring some sort of emergency response—were increasing. However, it may be that the workers' capacity to deal with the less worrying child care calls had also increased, rendering them less likely to need to present them. The third possibility is that workers were more ready to hear the abuse issue in an apparently less serious child care call.

The essential difference between the two kinds of calls would seem to be that in the desperate mothers who could not cope there remained some imaginative concern for a baby who could no longer be held or comforted, whereas in the abuse calls the situation was a more paranoid one in which the parent/child relation was dominated by fantasies of attack, the child's distress being experienced as a threat which must be destroyed. In such an emotional climate the parent retains little or no capacity to recognise the reality of the baby as a helpless and vulnerable being in need of care and attention.

Naturally, these modes of feeling coloured the relationship between worker and caller as well. The workers' image of themselves was of providing care and comfort but in the abuse calls they were sometimes required to assert firm structures and boundaries and confront the aggressive fantasies—a much more difficult task. To put the difference in a nutshell—in the child care calls there was a child who was out of control; in the abuse calls it was the parent who was out of control. Of course this distinction is by no means clear cut in most cases. However, a few calls illustrate the difference clearly and in the following examples it should be borne in mind that they have been selected for this purpose.

Ex 1 *Child Care Call* A woman with three children aged 7, 4 and 2 rang at the end of a long wet Sunday because the 4 year old girl was creating havoc. She had been playing up all day, screaming, destroying things, pulling down the curtains—rails and all. Now she was refusing to be put to bed and both parents were at the end of their tether. The family had been under a great strain recently as the husband had just started a new job after a period of unemployment.

The worker commiserated with the mother and then spoke to the child, singing her nursery rhymes down the phone. This lightened the atmosphere and the worker was able to draw the call to a close.

This appeared to be a family whose emotional resources had become seriously depleted but who, with a bit of input from a 'nursery rhyme auntie', were able to recover sufficiently to continue functioning.

Ex 2 *Child Abuse Call* The call was from a mother who 'loves her little girl but smacks her all the time'. The child was aged 4½ and wanted to please her mother all the time. There was another child of 2 years and the mother was 7 months pregnant. She was living with her boyfriend who was the father of all the children but gave her no encouragement and 'just goes off'. She then took it out on the little girl.

The phone call began with the caller saying 'I nearly bit my child'. She went on to describe having hit the child so hard that her face was bruised and the mother could not let her be seen outside. She spoke of a poor relationship with the boyfriend and with her own mother and also mentioned that she had lost a child who had died at birth. The 4½ year old was conceived very quickly afterwards.

The call lasted 45 minutes and ended with the caller saying 'Thank you for listening'.

The worker was left in tears and feeling that she had failed to confront the initial statement about the biting because she had been too frightened to do so.

When it is considered how difficult it is to take up such a blatant account of child abuse, both actual and threatened, in an anonymous phone call, the situation of social workers who are pilloried for failing to see what is before their eyes becomes more understandable, albeit not excusable. For the untrained volunteers of PA working in their own homes these difficulties are much harder to recognise let alone overcome. Whenever the phone rings there is the anxiety of not knowing what they will hear when they pick it up.

Although the incest calls and the hoax/fantasy calls were usually more extreme in content, the abuse calls were in one respect the most unnerving since alarm bells could be suddenly set ringing in the middle of an apparently innocuous call. And unlike, say the social services duty officer, the PA workers had no institutional structure which could be activated to deal with these potentially alarming situations. When these structures are absent it suddenly becomes very obvious how much containment they provide for the worker's anxieties. PA workers suffered enormously from the anxiety of being 'left with it all'.

Perhaps because they were so short on containment themselves they frequently failed to recognise the value of the containment they provided for their callers. Most of the child abuse callers were on the borderline between coping and not coping. They often appeared to be calling impulsively but of course, as we frequently pointed out, they had at least planned on the contingency of needing to call by having the phone number to hand. They called at the point when their resources would no longer stretch to meet the demands being made of them by their children. In other words, when the out of control child was in danger of activating the out of control child in themselves. For both the actual child and the internal child the common factor was the absence of a containing parent. Parents Anonymous offered to fill this gap, to be as it were anonymous parents.

The following 'typical' call illustrates well this perilous borderline between the out of control child and the out of control parent, as well as the parallel difficulty of distinguishing between an 'ordinary' child care call and a potentially dangerous situation of child abuse.

Ex 3 The caller, a woman of 23 years, married with a child of 3 and a year old baby rang about her 3 year old daughter. She described a chaotic, messy child who was creating havoc—e.g. pouring sugar on the floor and shampoo and lavatory cleaner in the bath. The caller had got so fed up she had put the children in the bath (with the shampoo and lavatory cleaner) and left them for a minute or two. When she returned the baby had slipped under the water and was drowning.

At this point the worker became very frightened but was able to put this back to the caller, saying 'that must have given you a bad fright' and went on to ask whether the caller was afraid of really hurting her child. The caller admitted that she had hit her 'too hard' at times, that

> she felt no love for her and was afraid of her being taken away. She had been to Child Guidance but they had been 'no good'. The worker, for lack of alternatives, encouraged her to return to Child Guidance and the caller agreed to give it another try.

The worker felt uncomfortable about pushing it back to Child Guidance but it seems likely that this was half in the caller's mind and by mentioning it she gave the worker the needed opportunity to encourage her. The worker made plain that she had received the message that the caller wished to convey, namely that her children were in danger and named Child Guidance as the appropriate place to deal with the problem.

The Child Care and Child Abuse calls, of which the three illustrated are fairly typical examples were well within the range of the worker's expectations. They were clearly the kind of situations for which PA was intended and therefore it might be thought that there would be a good fit between the callers' and workers' expectations of the service provided. Yet, despite the fact that many calls seemed to wind down naturally or end with the caller saying 'Thank you for listening', the workers were plagued with feelings of helplessness, inadequacy and guilt at their perceived failure to help. They felt they were doing the wrong thing, that they were the wrong person to help or were simply perplexed, left anxiously wondering 'What am I supposed to be doing?' We understood these reactions as vivid illustrations of counter-transference: the workers being made to feel what the callers felt in relation to their children. It was as though the callers were the crying babies and the workers the parents at the end of their tether, unable to pacify the child and doubting their own competence and resources in the face of the child's relentless onslaught of distress. Anonymous Parents indeed!

More disturbing still for the workers were those callers who induced a hostile reaction. One worker described wanting to give a caller a good shaking, another was horrified by her lack of sympathy for a caller who she could not be bothered with and simply wanted to get off the line. Could these reactions also be understood as counter-transference, reflecting either what the caller felt in relation to the actual child they were calling about or how, as a child themselves, they had experienced their own parents in relation to them—of both?

Looking at the worker's reactions to calls in terms of counter-transference also makes sense of their difficulty in confronting the possibility of abuse (e.g. Call 2). They often expressed the fear that the caller would hang up if they did so—and certainly there were occasions where this had happened. It was as though the workers became filled up with the callers own fears of their aggressive/destructive impulses and their potential consequences—either a dreadful explosion or abandonment and rejection. Ironically these fears underline the importance of being able to confront the feared abuse in order to provide, as anonymous parents, a model of a containing response to the feared—and fearful—out-of-control child.

Incest Calls

The child care/child abuse calls along with the problems-with-teenagers calls all shared a concern with common, perhaps universal parenting problems. As parents themselves the workers were able to make use of their own experience and operate on a tacit assumption of shared understanding. The basis for this work was 'Call us—we know what its like'. This approach has both strengths and limitations but at least it gave workers some sense of knowing what they were about, despite all the counter-transference factors and so on already described. No matter how serious the potential abuse the callers were at least sufficiently in touch with the emotional situation to make a call for help. None of the child abuse calls presented the bizarre features of deliberate sadistic cruelty characteristic of some of the horror stories which have featured so prominently in the popular press in recent years. The callers were not psychopathic and heartless but desperate and helpless in the face of their own damaging behaviour. To paraphrase George Bernard Shaw, they never abused a child except in hot blood. And in turn they made hot blooded contact with PA.

All this distinguished them from the incest callers who, apart from the hoax/fantasy callers, presented the PA workers with their greatest difficulties. They felt intuitively that the incest calls were 'different' and required a different response and we spent a lot of time looking at why this should be so.

One major difference is that in all the child abuse calls the abusers were women whereas in almost all the incest calls the abusers were men. Of course men do physically abuse their children but it seems they do not call PA. Nor apparently to their wives, although there were a few women callers who reported being assaulted by their husbands. (When men called regarding a child abuse problem the perpetrator was always a third party).

As almost all the PA workers are women (and none of the 'token' men came to the groups) the incest abusers presented an immediate barrier to understanding based on their own experience. But the main difference was a deeper, but also a more subtle one. Sexual abuse itself seems to be rooted in more disturbed—and disturbing—family relations and individual psychopathology. All parents must at some time at least have felt like hitting their children 'too hard' but all parents do not at some time feel like having sexual relations with their children. Indeed all of us in the workshop, members, leaders and back-ups alike had to struggle with feelings of outrage, revulsion and disgust at something which felt unthinkable, something which even when brought to our attention we would have much preferred not to think about. Sexual abuse itself crosses a barrier both social and psychological and while labelling it may not help us to understand, it does at least help us to recognise it if we call that barrier by its traditional name—*taboo*.

Most of the incest callers were men who were abusing their daughters to a greater or lesser degree. The daughters ranged in age from 4½ to 27 but most were roughly at the age of puberty (10–14). These men were sufficiently concerned about what they were doing to call PA—in fact one or two were in a state of deep anguish. But their concern had a different, more schizoid quality from the 'ordinary' child abuse callers. The incest abusers presented themselves almost as helpless onlookers at behaviour which with another part of themselves they enjoyed and wanted to continue. This distinguished them straight away from the women who were hitting their children all of whom wanted more or less desperately to stop. (One exception highlights the rule—the woman who used PA as a stick to beat the child with, saying to the child as she hung up 'Right, they'll come for you tomorrow'.) The difficulty with the incest abusers was that they *said* they wanted to stop but clearly had no real intention of doing so. One man was able to put the dilemma quite clearly—and it is no coincidence that he was the most anguished of all the callers we heard about.

> He had begun 'messing around' with his 11 year old daughter and was 'horrified' that this might lead to intercourse. He was in despair because he knew that if his wife found out it would be the end of the marriage and of him. Yet when the worker asked if this were not enough to stop him he replied 'No, because at the time the sexual satisfaction is more important than anything else. It is a sexual pleasure better than anything else I have ever known'.

In order to mainain this split in themselves—as part and parcel of it—these callers kept themselves eerily distanced from the consequences of their behaviour. They demonstrated a discomforting absence of the revulsion which we all took to be natural and intrinsic to family life. One man who had been having sex with his 12 year old daughter for some time had noticed that she was becoming 'a bit moody'. He thought the sexual relationship 'might be upsetting her' and phoned to ask about this. It is difficult to know how to relate to someone who demonstrates such psychopathic insensitivity.

One further difference between the two groups is perhaps the most fundamental of all in that it concerns the roots of their abusing behaviour and by implication the means by which they can be helped—or not. The women who hit their children were not only distressed by what they had done; their behaviour was itself a direct expression of the emotional distress they were in at the time. Their behaviour was essentially *impulsive*. Unable to control the raging child within them they turned to PA in the hope of finding some containment to compensate for the lack of containment within themselves and their immediate environment. They could therefore often be helped by a nurturing response which provided understanding, reassurance and support.

The men sexually abusing their daughters, however, only experienced remorse afterwards and sometimes not even then. They were not in distress at the time—precisely the opposite: they were enjoying themselves, however perversely. Their behaviour was essentially *compulsive*. They were driven to it not by their distress but as a means of *avoiding* distress—i.e. the perverse sexual act is a way of blotting out and/or attempting to master unbearable pain and anxiety but as this is always unsuccessful it has to be endlessly, and compulsively, repeated. This explains the abusers' unnerving lack of anxiety about the damage they might be inflicting on their victims—in stark contrast to the abusing women who were usually crippled by sometimes quite unrealistic anxieties about their destructiveness. Thus, reassurance and support was the last thing the incest abusers needed. Nor, in most cases, did the workers stand any chance at all of being able to speak to the underlying pain and anxiety—even for experienced psychotherapists the sexual abuser is one of the most difficult types of patients to reach. Therefore, the only positive intervention the PA workers could hope to make was to confront the incest abusers with the reality of the consequences of their behaviour in terms of the effect incest has on its victims subsequent development and to issue a firm 'No!'. The workers had to put aside the role of nurturer and carer and take up a sterner stance of the authority that proscribes. They needed to stand for the upholding of the taboo and state clearly to the callers: 'this must stop'. In doing so they would also be blocking the collusive seduction into which many of these callers sought to lure them.

According to traditional role expectations it is the mother who provides nurture and care and the father who represents authority and says 'No'. The PA workers, women themselves, often felt themselves bound by these expectations. However, the incest calls provided intriguing evidence that in this area it may be the mother's role to say 'No!' to the father's illicit attempts to seek nurture in inappropriate sexual contact with their daughters. It was notable that in a number of the incest calls the mother was either absent or dead. This would suggest that even where the incest taboo has not been internalised it can be maintained by the mother's presence. Indeed it is often suggested that even when mothers are present, incest cannot take place without their collusion. In such cases the PA workers might represent the absent mothers and issue an external prohibition on their behalf.

There is also, of course, the parallel possibility that it is the absence of the nurture provided by the mother which provokes the tipping over into an enactment of incest. In fact, cases where the mother had died provided a significant qualification to the prevailing condemnation felt for the incest abusers. Often it seemed that father and daughter took consolation in each other in the wake of their grief, only later awakening to the consequences of what they had done. There were calls from fathers who were now trying to extricate themselves from their teenage daughters rather than the other way round. And the saddest case of all was the man who felt that he had brought a new bloom of happiness into the bleak life of his mentally handicapped 27 year old daughter. Nevertheless, while these cases aroused a more compassionate response and often called for more gentle handling, the basic issue was the same: it is the responsibility of the parent, not the child, to ensure that the taboo is kept.

Saying 'No!' did not come easily to the PA workers since it was at odds with how they saw PA and their role within it. PA was set up to support parents and it took some time to get across the idea that saying 'No' could be a form of support. Initially they felt caught in a trap of feeling guilty if they did express their condemnation and impotent if they did not.

They were also afraid of alienating the caller and thereby losing what was probably the only tenuous link to helping the victim. This anxiety, however, carried with it the risk of colluding with the abuser. In the second series of workshops one very competent worker described a contact with an incest caller which had been going on for well over a year.

> This man was abusing his 4 year old daughter (touching her and masturbating) taking his opportunity on evenings when his wife was out. He would call the PA worker at these times, and she would spend long periods on the phone with him being encouraged to believe that in so doing she was preventing him molesting his daughter. Sometimes he would be unable to control himself any longer and would slam the phone down. Much of the conversation concerned the caller's unhappy psycho-

> sexual history on which the worker attempted to counsel him. Eventually she persuaded him to see a psychiatrist specialising in incest but when the psychiatrist insisted on knowing the man's name and address he stopped going, and also stopped phoning. The worker then felt left with all the guilt and all the anxiety.

The psychiatrist had called the man's bluff about his real wish to be helped. Some members of the group felt this was wrong—what about the poor girl? But others pointed out that the PA worker had been working with the man anonymously for eighteen months and that hadn't stopped the incest either. All that had been achieved was that, as one astute member put it, the caller had off-loaded his responsibility onto the worker. She carried his conscience, his anxiety and his guilt and this left him free to carry on.

During the course of the workshop this caller made contact again. On this occasion the worker took a very different line, insisting he sought professional help, refusing to act as a channel of confession and pointing out to him in graphic terms the potential psychological damage suffered by incest victims. This left him 'deep in thought' but the worker felt he was too self-preoccupied to take much heed. Nevertheless she felt extremely relieved by what she had done.

Although the worker's refusal to collude with the caller any longer might not in itself have stopped the incest it did confront both parties with some very uncomfortable feelings which needed to be faced if any change were to take place. The worker was faced with the limits of what could be offered and the consequent feelings of failure and impotence. The caller was faced with his own reponsibility for his actions and left to consider their consequences.

Incest and Fantasy—an uncomfortable boundary

Several similar themes emerged in another long-term call which dominated the first series of workshops. Ironically, this call was from an incest victim, a teenage girl of around 14 years called 'Jenny'.

This was the first incest call presented and it became the focus for all of the first group's anxieties about working in this difficult area, placing the worker in the unenviable position of carrying the group's collective sense of responsibility in addition to her own. The fact that the call concerned such an ostensibly innocent victim made these feelings all the more acute: many of the members, including the worker concerned, had teenage daughters of their own.

> Jenny had been calling PA for over a year. At first she would simply cry down the phone and was unable to talk. Gradually the worker was able to win her confidence and coax her into speaking. It was a long time before she 'came out with it and said her father had had sex with her'. After that she would frequently phone in tears after such occasions. The worker had worked hard at trying to find an appropriate referral for the girl and had eventually made contact with a sympathetic psychiatrist. The girl kept one appointment but then failed to keep the next. At the point the work was first presented she had just phoned to say that the reason she had not kept the appointment was that she had taken an overdose and been in hospital.

In retrospect, it is possible to see the element of blackmail in this girl's behaviour and the way she kept the worker bound to her by provoking anxiety and guilt. Although she was ostensibly phoning for help the worker felt caught up in a secret complicity with her, one which she desperately wanted to break but from which she could see no way out. In other words the caller was making the worker feel exactly how an incest victim might feel in relation to the abuser. The worker felt paralysed by PA's policy of confidentiality (of which Jenny knew) and by the fear of what disclosure, even if it were possible, might do to the family.

The girl's ambivalence regarding disclosure was clear: why else had she chosen PA with whom she could remain safely anonymous?

Her motives, however, were less obviously understood and the various possibilities discussed in the group proved highly contentious, especially the suggestion that she might, in part, be enjoying the incest herself. Against this, it was suggested that the father's threats and the real likelihood of breaking up the family were quite sufficient as explanations of her dilemma.

The work with this caller spanned almost the entire life of the first series of workshops as the developing saga was brought back 4 or 5 times. There was a tremendous feeling of impotence combined with a feeling that something must be done—but what, and by whom? It turned out that the girl had, apparently by chance, given the worker her telephone number. Was it appropriate for her act on this and try and make contact with the parents or should the psychiatrist—who had the girl's full name and address—be the one to act, and if so, how?

Up until this point the difficulties in the work with this caller were similar to those in the work with the man who was abusing his 4 year old daughter. There was the urgent feeling of wanting to intervene to stop the incest combined with feelings of powerlessness to do so; the attempt at referral to an apparently more powerful professional who then gets embroiled in the same difficulties; the difficulty of relating to ambivalent feelings regarding the incest; and the unwitting collusion whereby the worker is caught up in the caller's own feelings and perpetuates their ambivalence.

However, at this point an important element entered into the work with Jenny which was not (apparently) present in the case of the abuser, This element can be summed up in one word: incredulity.

The issues so far described may be highlighted in telephone work but they are not specific to it. Most 'front-line' workers, (e.g. social workers, GPs or health visitors) must have experienced similar dilemmas and difficulties at some time. But for these workers the physical presence of the client or patient immediately sets them in a context of social reality and acts as a balance to the world of feelings and fantasies with which workers inevitably—and often appropriately—get caught up. For workers whose only contact with 'clients' is via the telephone, all these physical cues and clues are missing; they are wide open to receive the caller's story exactly as *they* relate it. This is their strength and their weakness. It enables them to get right into a caller's world with an unusual degree of immediacy but it deprives them of the means by which some bridge might be made between the caller's world and external reality (i.e. shared, social reality). So long as the callers themselves are rooted in some shared reality this is not a problem. But there are some situations in which it becomes *the* dominant issue. To put it bluntly, how do you know if the caller is telling the truth?

The only obvious guide for the PA worker is whether the caller's story sounds credible. But is this a reliable guide? After all truth is stranger than fiction and there are more things in heaven and earth then were in Horatio's philosophy. When the workers found themselves up against horrific stories of cruelty and abuse it could have been only too comforting to believe that they were untrue, that the call was a 'hoax' call but how could one be sure?

When Jenny was first presented to the group one member questioned the veracity of her story. The worker replied 'I had doubts. I had a lot of doubts but I really believe in her (because of the way she came out with it). At the beginning I must admit I thought, has she? But not when she's gone to see the doctor, plus the fact that he believes her, plus the fact that she had cigarette burns she'd never mentioned to me but the doctor had actually seen them'.

All this seemed fairly conclusive at the time and the issue was dropped. But when with our encouragement the worker and the psychiatrist took steps to intervene and bring matters to a head the reality of Jenny's story began to crumble away as all the apparently 'hard' information turned out to be false trails. There was no record of the overdose, which school she went to and the name and address she had given the psychiatrist were false. For a while there was still the telephone number but when the psychiatrist contacted social services, who contacted the police, who traced the number this turned out to be not Jenny's number but a 'friend'.

The group was stunned. The worker felt that Jenny had made her 'feel like an idiot' and she stopped coming to the group for some time, perhaps too humiliated—or too angry—to face us. She felt she could not trust or believe anything anyone said. Other workers said they would doubt every call from now on: 'You get this question mark and you wonder "how many others?" '

The sense of reality dissolving around us was so great that one of the leaders questioned whether the caller really was a 14 year old girl, temporarily forgetting that the psychiatrist had actually seen her. Yet the fact of her having lied about her identifying details did not necessarily mean that her story was untrue, merely that its truth could not be proven. But might this not be exactly how the girl herself might feel especially as she claimed to have told her mother at one point who had said 'Don't be so stupid'. The recent publicity about sexual abuse has stressed again and again how difficult it is for incest victims to get people to believe their stories. Secondly, the lying might have been an expression of her ambivalence about disclosure. Thirdly, and most worrying, was the possibility that the group's feeling of unreality was a reflection of the girls own sickness. If this girl was living in a fantasy world then we had all been living in it too and taking it for reality. But even if her story was true—might she not sometimes feel that her experience could not be real, unable to accept the enormity of what was being done to her in the name of love? The sense of unreality, the doubting of perceptions would then constitute an extreme form of denial. In other words might it not sometimes be preferable to think oneself mad than acknowledge that what is unbearable and unthinkable is real?

Eventually this caller was traced via the friend whose phone she had used. The psychiatrist visited the house with the police. The father said it was all lies and the girl herself denied it all. The family details she had given, for example about her siblings, were all false. Nevertheless the father admitted that he had once 'touched her underneath the breast in play' and the psychiatrist was left with the impression, despite the girl saying 'I made it all up', that her story was indeed true. He planned to continue to see her at school but, he said, 'phone therapy is not going to work'.

As well as being a fascinating and gripping story in itself with many features of a detective thriller, this call serves to illustrate the complexities and confusions in dealing with so-called 'hoax' calls. Despite their doubts, the workers continued to be taken in repeatedly by callers whose tales were far more bizarre and far less believable than Jenny. Only a few calls were unequivocal hoaxes—usually from male callers who turned out to be telephone masturbators. Others were 'found out' when they made many repeat calls to different workers, either peddling the same story or a similar version of it. But many calls existed in a 'grey area' where workers were willing to give callers the benefit of the doubt for fear of turning away callers who were genuinely seeking help in a desperate situation. The example of Jenny where the question was never fully resolved showed how finely balanced the discrimination of fantasy and reality could be. When asked how they *knew* a call was genuine there was general agreement to one worker's reply that 'you just have to believe'.

Unfortunately belief, or more accurately, the suspension of disbelief, entailed the risk of being hoodwinked, exploited, disgusted and humiliated. Nor should it be thought that only untrained volunteers could get themselves into such a mess. The group leaders were equally vulnerable to being taken in by stories which turned out subsequently to be untrue.

The most spectacular example of this occurred in the second series of workshops. In one group a call was presented from a suicidal 12 year old girl whose mother had died and whose father was sexually abusing her. She had called again the following night, with slurred speech, asking 'how many pills does it take to kill yourself?' and eventually dropping the phone, having apparently lost consciousness. Understandably the worker was left extremely distressed by this call and the group became preoccupied with the need to trace the caller. One member suggested the call might be a hoax but the others were aghast at the suggestion and it was rejected, even though one of the back-ups mentioned a similar call he had been involved with over the weekend which, it turned out, was simultaneously being discussed in the other group. This call was from a 12 year old American girl who told a horrific story of her mother and boyfriend being dead in the next room. The call had gone on for four hours with gory details slowly spilling out about incest and murder. This girl was also suicidal and attempts had been made to trace her by contacting the police and tapping the phone but her identity remained uncertain (shades of Jenny).

When yet another call was mentioned from a 13 year old American girl whose mother drank and had boyfriends and who shrieked when the worker mentioned her father, we began to feel that we were getting ensnared in a most bizarre and complex fantasy world by a very disturbed caller who might well not be a 12/13 year old at all.

The following week we arranged for both groups to meet together in an attempt to restore our collective sanity. Feelings ran very high throughout the session and we were left amazed at the power of this caller to invade and take over so many lives and so much time.

There was some evidence from one of the back-ups that this caller was also well known to the Samaritans *who had instructed their volunteers not to deal with her*. This raised for PA the whole question of its need for organisational polices and guidelines, to give the workers some structure within which they could assert their own boundaries. This was one of the most important issues to come out of our overall work with PA—and it is therefore discussed at greater length in Chapter 5, the Professionalisation of Parents Anonymous.

Without some assertion of structure and boundary the group oscillated wildly between belief and disbelief. For example, one of the leaders became convinced that one of the calls (the overdose girl) *was* genuine at exactly the same moment the other became convinced that it was not. This quality of 'switching convictions' between what is real and what is fantasy is what produces the sense of craziness in working with these callers.

We were able to identify another important and closely related feature of these hoax, or as we preferred to call them, fantasy calls: they drive the workers to break the rules. 'To hell with anonymity', as one worker said, in the desperate bid to pursue the 'truth', as if the truth—if it could be discovered—would restore sanity. But the reality is that these callers themselves are almost certainly unable to distinguish fantasy from reality and this is what gets induced in the workers.

As already mentioned, the absence of concrete physical cues make telephone help-line workers especially vulnerable to this difficulty. Nevertheless, we believe it too is not specific to telephone work but is indicative of the intrinsically problematic nature of the distinction between fantasy and reality. As soon as psychic reality is accorded a status equivalent with material reality, 'objective' evidence (i.e. verifiable by reference to the material world) ceases to be a universally valid touchstone of what is real and what is not.

On this point we found ourselves curiously united with the PA workers despite the enormous differences in our working task since, as psychotherapists, we face an analogous dilemma in the hermetic environment of the consulting room. Although we have the patient physically present in the room, our information about his life outside the consulting room rests entirely on what he tells us. Some psychotherapists have attempted to resolve this difficulty by treating all their patients' communications in the 'as if' mode, i.e. as though they are fantasies. This has some validity in so far as the psychotherapist's concern is with the imaginal world and he or she deliberatrly sets out to create an environment in which imaginal reality can be explored. Even so, the question of the relative weight to be assigned to fantasy versus reality has been a subject of furious debate in the psychoanalytic world since its inception. And it is surely significant that not only this debate but psychoanalysis itself emerged out of the thorny arena of sexual abuse.

It will be recalled that Freud at first took literally his patients' stories of having been seduced in childhood. The decisive step for the creation of psychoanalysis was the moment when he came to believe that these stories were in fact wishful fantasies. Out of this imaginative leap came the theory of infantile sexuality, the oedipus complex, the clue to understanding the phenomenon of transference and, perhaps in the long run most significant of all, the notion of unconscious fantasy. This view has not gone unchallenged however. In the 1950s John Bowlby pointed to the importance of the child's real experience of attachment and separation in the genesis of neurotic disturbance, against what he saw as the excessive importance Melanie Klein and her followers were giving to unconscious fantasy. More recently the wheel has turned full circle as Jeffrey Masson has argued that Freud was right in the first place and the edifice of psychoanalysis since his rejection of the seduction theory is nothing but a massive testament to his failure of moral courage. (Masson 1984). This view is echoed in more temperate form by many of those now campaigning against sexual abuse who maintain, with Masson, that analysts and therapists have been too quick to disbelieve their patients' stories as fantasies when current evidence suggests that sexual abuse is far more widespread than has ever been imagined.

Be that as it may, our experience with PA suggests that caution is necessary in this area. It is worth pointing out that one of the main reasons why sexual abuse of children is so traumatic is because of what it does to their unconscious fantasies. That is, it is destructive of the necessary imaginal psychic space which children need in order to develop their emotional and relational life, that which Winnicott called the third area of transitional phenomena or the location of cultural experience (Winnicott 1971). It is interesting to note that Jung, with his emphasis on the importance of myth and fantasy also fell out with Freud over the incest question but in his case it was because he argued that Freud took incest fantasies *too* literally (Jung 1912/1952). A Jungian view of the problem therefore might suggest that incest fantasies are archetypal in origin and the danger of enacting them is that they produce an eruption of archetypal material into consciousness with which the child is unable to cope. This might go some way to explaining the disturbing blur between the genuine incest victim and the apparently psychotic or near-psychotic fantasy callers.

However, this is not the place to adjudicate on this debate even if such adjudication were possible. The main point I want to make is that in the area of sexuality and of incest in particular, fantasy and reality are inextricably linked. All of us have difficulties in sorting out the one from the other, not just psychotherapists, PA workers and their callers.

CHAPTER THREE

Why Parents Anonymous?

The prime importance of good diagnostic assessment in short-term therapeutic work is well-known. The same applies to the usually very brief, often one-off contacts that the PA workers had with their callers. However, whereas assessment normally requires a high level of skill, the PA workers discovered with us that understanding the reasons why people called *them*, i.e. PA rather than some other agency, revealed a great deal of what they needed to know in order to help them. This was because what they were *not* there to do was *solve the problem*. Clearly this is impossible in one or two telephone conversations with a stranger and therefore too great a preoccupation on its roots and branches was likely to be a distraction from PA's central task. The trouble was, the workers were far from clear exactly what that central task was.

Our task as trainers was firstly to help them identify their task and then to help them to stick to it.

We identified four reasons why people called PA which taken together describe the kind of service an anonymous helpline like PA provides for the community.

1. *Anonymity*

This has already been mentioned in terms of the way callers used Parents Anonymous as Anonymous Parents. Here it is only necessary to add that the fantasies callers had about these anonymous parents had both a general and a specific nature, i.e. each caller related to the anonymous voice at the other end of the phone in terms of their own image of a parent figure. In other words anonymity provided a ready made vehicle for transference projections, (the making of the worker into the likeness of a figure in the caller's own psyche).

For example:

> A caller ostensibly called about her poor relationship with her children but threw in at the end of the call that 'yesterday was the anniversary of

> my mother's death'. The worker was left feeling that she had missed the central issue until it was too late and found herself pining for the caller, regretting her feelings of irritation towards her earlier in the call. In this case the disembodied voice on the telephone—so near and yet so far—seemed a most apt representation of the absent, dead mother with whom the caller wanted, albeit ambivalently, to be in contact. And, of course, the worker's response provided a vivid reflection of what the caller might now feel about the mother with whom she had missed the central issue until it was too late.

The same process operated in a more negative form in the hoax and fantasy calls, particularly with sex callers (not all of whom were overt telephone masturbators). Here the caller used the telephone link in a narcissistic way—the worker's voice not representing a person with whom a relationship could be made, however tenuous and overlaid with transference and ambivalence, but merely something to be appropriated into the caller's own fantasy system, exploited without regard to the worker's own existence and then discarded.

For callers who were abusing their children, their own anonymity may have been of greater significance than that of the worker. Many of the child abuse callers were deeply afraid of having their children taken away from them if what they were doing became known to 'the authorities'. This clearly made PA a preferable option to any of the statutory services. For the sexual abuser too there was the fear of the consequences if they were discovered—the potential break-up of the family and a possible prison sentence for themselves. While to some extent these fears also have a transference element in them they are clearly realistic.

Here anonymity means confidentiality and this regularly faced the workers with a much more difficult dilemma than that generally faced by the Samaritans or Childline who also offer confidentiality as a feature of their service. By and large the Samaritans are dealing with callers who are at risk to themselves—they are their own victims. Childline are dealing with those who are the victims of others. PA, however, dealt (and deals) with people who were putting others at risk—the abused child. How far was it right that the caller's anonymity be protected at the expense of his or her victim? The aim of PA was to 'break the cycle of child abuse', and yet often it seemed that the service functioned for the benefit of the abusers. We have seen the sort of difficulties this could create in the incest abuser call from the second series of workshops. But this also illustrated that if the caller wants to be known they will make it possible to trace them. If not, then however painful for the worker, it is unlikely that they can be helped any further than the constraints of a telephone call allow. For better or worse the confidentiality and anonymity of the service gives callers a very high degree of control over it—all they have to do is put down the phone.

For some callers the control must in itself have been reassuring since loss of control was exactly their problem. Although we tended to focus on the callers' fear of the statutory services there must also have been for many a high degree of *shame* that can be especially imagined for those callers who were themselves supposed to be helping others—social workers and health visitors were among those who called PA for personal, not professional reasons. Shame is a very difficult emotion to define, especially its distinction from guilt, but one of its characteristic features is that it involves being *seen by others*. Sartre's famous example of the man peeping through a keyhole points this up: he only feels ashamed when he realises that someone is observing him. At this moment his sense of control over his own self-perception seeps away into the other (Sartre 1969). To be unseen and anonymous mitigates the shame of admitting to behaviour that falls below the expected standard. The statutory services tended to be seen by both worker and caller alike as the representatives of social expectations and PA represented a more allowing and less humiliating alternative—and one which the caller could control.

2. *Ambivalence*

Closely linked to the anonymity of the service is the callers' ambivalence about seeking help. Again this was a notable feature of both the incest abuser and Jenny. Anyone seeking help has to overcome a certain degree of ambivalence for which there are many causes—e.g. fear of exposure, fear of dependency, reluctance to admit there is a problem, loss of pride in one's ability to cope, fear of condemnation etc. Some people are driven to seek help by the urgency of their need even when ambivalence is very great, others may feel that on balance they would rather stay with the problem than go through the trauma of seeking help. An agency like PA offers a compromise for people who are caught on the horns of this dilemma: not only does the help offered remain under their control but its limitations, so frustrating to the worker, are built into the structure and provide the ambivalent caller with a way of seeking help and not 'really' seeking help at the same time.

Ambivalence was a common feature of all types of calls received by PA and I have therefore chosen an illustration from one of the types of call not so far discussed—problems with teenagers.

A man called about his 17 year old step-son who was sniffing butane gas and had a history of trouble including violence and arson. The caller wanted a referral to a 'specialist'. When the worker attempted to find out something about the family she was met with blanket denials that anything was wrong. The caller was simultaneously conducting a conversation with other members of the family, relaying what was said both ways. An air of levity prevailed.

Clearly the ambivalence here is the familiar one of a family being reluctant to admit that the 'identified patient' in the family is a scapegoat for the whole family's problems. The worker felt angry and critical towards the caller for not taking the problem seriously and not listening to her. Similarly the family appeared unable to 'listen' to the significance of their son's behaviour. Phoning PA offered an easy option by which they could appear to be doing something about it. Whether they would actually have the commitment to follow through a referral seemed highly unlikely.

Some callers were already receiving help from professional agencies such as social services or child guidance clinics. The PA workers reactions to such calls ranged from perplexity to irritation. They could not understand why people who were already receiving help from the professionals should need their help as well. This had a lot to do with their idealised image of the professionals which is discussed in Chapter 5. However sometimes this image would swing to its opposite, as such polar extremes are inclined to do, and then professionals would be criticised and denigrated for their uselessness and failure to respond. In all this there was a great tendency for collusion with the callers' very similar attitudes of ambivalence towards professionals. The example presented earlier of the woman whose baby nearly drowned demonstrated how, almost by accident, the worker was able to resist this collusion. It will be recalled that the caller had been to Child Guidance and found them 'no good'. Nevertheless she succeeded in inducing in the worker such alarm that the worker was left in no doubt that professional help was necessary and advised her to return to Child Guidance 'for lack of alternatives'. She thereby used whatever little influence she had to weight the caller's ambivalence towards the need to seek appropriate help, despite her resistance, hostility and—who knows?—perhaps valid reservations about the help offered.

This is an example of a most useful function which PA can fulfil as auxiliaries to the professionals precisely because they themselves are outside the professional network and closer to the clients' world.

Not all the callers who were involved with professional agencies could be referred back there, however. Some were amongst that sad group of clients known to every front-line agency who could not really be helped, either because they were too damaged, or too ambivalent. For these people PA offered some respite in a crisis but like everyone else they could offer no more. We suspected that many of the fantasy callers also came into this category.

Finally the theme of ambivalence is linked to the workers' fear of confrontation mentioned earlier. Although in part this was for fear of what they might hear it was also the fear of confronting the callers' ambivalence. Several callers did in fact hang up in affronted fury when workers pressed them to seek further help or put into words the avoided issue. The question 'why PA?' was particularly valuable here in that it could alert workers to a hidden issue of child abuse in a call where it might otherwise be missed. The caller who nearly bit her child (p 15) had announced this in the first sentence and then gone on to talk about her own situation and past history. The worker had been diverted by all this but was then left with the feeling of having failed to confront the abuse.

In fact this caller's presentation demonstrated not only her ambivalence but also the reason for it. It was as though she was saying 'I want you to attend to the fact that I am abusing my child but I need you to understand my own situation and to treat me sympathetically—i.e. don't abuse *me*!' This was typical of the need with many callers to relate to both sides in them—the abuser *and* the abused.

Nevertheless, we also took a firm line on this issue, recommending confrontation even at the risk of losing the caller, since the alternative risked colluding with the avoidance of the problem. Of course confrontation must be handled carefully and sensitively but we felt that even where callers hung up something may have been achieved in that the unmentionable had at least been mentioned:

> One worker was almost ashamed to tell us about the male caller with two daughters, aged 18 and 16. He had been sexually abusing the elder one, but had now sent her away to live with her grandmother. Spontaneously the worker said crossly 'and now I suppose you're going to start on the younger one!'. The caller promptly hung up but perhaps the message had got across.

3. *Instant Response*

No other form of help is as instantly available as a telephone helpline. Even the most accessible face-to-face help requires either the helped or the helper to make a journey to the place where the other is. In most cases there are receptionists and appointments to negotiate and all the feelings that arouses of the 'too busy' inaccessible professional. (Voluntary counselling agencies such as Relate : Marriage Guidance are, in this sense, highly professionalised with waiting lists of up to three months).

With a telephone helpline however, it is not just an appointment or temporary holding operation at the other end of the phone but the real thing—the help being offered is immediately there. The entire paraphernalia of gate-keeping functions with which professionals surround themselves in order to protect their boundaries has been removed. It is therefore only a small step from feeling that there are no boundaries of *access* to the help offered to feeling that the help offered is itself boundless.

Unfortunately this is far from the case. The telephone which removes the access boundary simultaneously imposes boundaries of its own—e.g. the lack of face to face contact and all the possibilities for an exchange of human warmth which go with it. Sometimes PA workers felt intense frustration that they could not give their callers a hug, or hold their hands while they cried. (Ironically, many professionals eschew physical contact with their clients, as a way of protecting the boundaries of the relationship).

Telephone calls have, in fact, a built-in boundary in that they are communication at a distance. This factor is yet another feature of the multi-faceted ambivalence of callers, and perhaps of workers too, towards making close relationships with each other. On the one hand it would *seem* as though they were very close to each other as they were in a sense in each others homes. In reality what was in each others homes was a voice rounded out into an imaginary presence. Jenny and her worker for example described their imaginary images of what each other looked like. Jenny's image of her worker was completely 'out' and as far as the worker's image of Jenny. . .

Nevertheless, so long as the limitations of this form of instant response are kept in mind it has a great deal to offer which again cannot be provided by the professional network of services. Some callers did not need professional help but were simply in the midst of a crisis which made them feel at the end of their tether *now* but might look very different in the morning. A good example of this was the first example given of a Child Care call—the 'nursery-rhyme auntie'. A call to social services in similar circumstances might have elicited a quite inappropriate response. By the time the slow grinding wheels of a large bureaucracy had lumbered into action producing a social work visit the need would have passed. Yet, once started, this large machine may be difficult to stop. How many social workers would risk closing the case on the spot without conducting further investigations? The alternative is that in a hard-pressed department such cases would not even get a look in.

The PA workers sometimes discovered to their cost how short-lived an intense crisis could be. Worried themselves, they would call back a day or so later to the bitterly depressed mother who could not cope a minute longer only to hear a cheerful voice on the other end of the phone saying 'Parents Who? Oh yes—everything is fine now'. In some cases this might well have been due to a denial of her problem, the other pole of the caller's ambivalence having gained precedence in the meantime. But in others it was due to the worker's own (unrecognised) effectiveness in containing the crisis. Psychotherapists and counsellors know that sometimes a very distressed client can be helped simply by offering a home phone number which does not actually have to be used. It is very likely that many potential PA callers use the phone number in the same way, having it to hand as an insurance policy for a rainy day. When it really buckets down it may be very reassuring to make a claim and discover that the insurance company of anonymous parents pays out instantly with no questions asked.

PA's instant availability in time of crisis or emergency was of value not only to those who did not need professional help but also to those who were already receiving it. Professionals by and large set their own agendas, responding in their own way in their own time. Indeed sociologists have argued that this characteristic of defining the client's problem for him rather than accepting his prior definition is constitutive of professional activity (Marshall, 1963, quoted in Wilding, 1982). As Haug and Susman (1969-70) put it 'the right to define the nature of the client's problem is the core of the professional's autonomy' (quoted in Wilding, op. cit.).

From the professional's point of view this amounts to no more than a definition of appropriate boundaries of relevant expertise. However it is important to recognise that it may appear in quite another guise to the client. Although the wish for instant and boundless help undoubtedly contributes to clients' ambivalence in that it is bound to be frustrated, there may be times when instant help is genuinely needed. The irony is, as previously indicated, that instant help is actually more limited in what it can offer than help which is structured by professional boundaries. Such boundaries not only limit availability but by the same token guarantee a space within which work can be done. I am reminded of the scene in Alan Bleasdale's play *Yosser's Story* when Yosser bursts in on his psychiatrist while she is interviewing another patient, demanding to know where his children are. (They had been taken into care). It is the other patient who protests that he is interrupting *her* time.

PA's role in such a crisis could thus be described as taking care of the Yossers of this world until the relevant professional is available.

For example:

A Zimbabwian woman, single mother with 18 month and 4 month old children. She had been a student in the UK for ten years and called in great distress because she had just received a letter from the Home Office requiring her to leave without delay. She had a social worker but had not been able to reach her and had also tried to get in touch with the Law Centre but without success. The worker made a few practical suggestions and offered to phone back the following day. When she did so the caller was much calmer.

The interesting thing about this call was the hints of a hidden child care (or abuse) problem which it was not necessary to take up. Why was there a social worker involved? Why call PA who clearly could not do anything about the very real presenting problem? Nevertheless, the worker had offered to contain the anxiety and reassure, until the appropriate agencies were available. As she said, 'As a volunteer I'm prepared to do that'.

We also thought it might have been helpful to the caller that the worker did *not* know the whole story of why she had a social worker. At such times the important thing for the caller is to find someone who will be unequivocably on their side.

4. *Listening*

Listening is an underrated activity. It is so basic to all forms of help that its value often goes unrecognised. Listening is the *sine qua non* of a telephone help-line; it is what PA was primarily set up to do, yet the workers found it hard to grasp that listening is actually a form of help in itself. They felt instead that they needed to *do* something and were plagued by feelings of inadequacy often because there simply was nothing they *could* do—except listen. After all the caller was an anonymous stranger at a distance with whom they were linked only by the fragile thread of telecommunication. Yet it took one of the least sophisticated members of the group, to say 'but listening is a useful thing'.

Much of the difficulty in valuing their listening stemmed from a difficulty in valuing themselves and what they had to offer. Again this is closely connected with the relationship to the professionals who were seen as having all the resources. When we had our first review of the workshop the group was fulsome in its praise for *us* as 'absolutely fantastic listeners'.

Of course self-confidence is easier for professionals who are at least in part able to rely on their training and expertise to reassure them of their value. A good doctor knows she must listen to the patient if she wants to make the best possible diagnosis and indeed there may be times when she too can *only* listen, e.g. when patients have a terminal illness. But there is a massive array of interventions which are availabe to her at other times and it is not unreasonable, indeed, it is essential, that she should take some respite in their use. More subtly the psychotherapist or counsellor whose stock in trade is listening also has at his disposal his knowledge of theory and technique and the range of interventions which issue from that. He may need to be circumspect about when and how he interprets but there is no doubt that interpretation can be used as a form of 'doing something' and it is only the rare master of the art who can truly eschew all such reassuring activity.

The only analogous activity available to PA was the giving of practical advice and information. This was one of their legitimate functions and there were some calls which could be dealt with entirely on this level. For this purpose each PA worker had a directory of relevant services and agencies and they varied in the use they made of it. Those callers who could be dealt with in this 'cut and dried' way obviously tended not to find their way into the group, although when such calls were presented they were often not as cut and dried as might first have been thought.

Similarly there were calls when either the workers or the caller—or both—had attempted to maintain a practical focus but had been left frustrated and dissatisfied.

Our view was that while practical advice and information had a role to play in the service PA offered, the agency's main function was the provision of a 'listening ear'. Once workers allowed themselves to be diverted from that focus, confusion and uncertainty prevailed.

It is now a rather outmoded cliché in social work practice that practical presenting problems are often a screen or ticket of entry for underlying emotional difficulties. The inherent danger of this view is that genuine practical difficulties will be cast aside as the workers pursue their appetite for more 'juicy' emotional conflicts.

This danger is particularly serious in an agency such as a social service department which controls access to a wide range of practical resources but is frequently deluged by a level of genuine material deprivation which far outstrips the department's capacity to respond. In such circumstances concentrating on emotional problems can become a convenient deflection of material demands.

The situation is very different for PA whose only practical resource is information, either about other agencies or perhaps about issues connected with child rearing (e.g. the role of diet in hyper-active children). Frequently callers requesting information turned out to already possess all the information which PA could provide. What then were they really asking for by ringing PA?

> A woman called about her 3 year old son who was having enormous tantrums. The worker responded with a standard pack of practical advice—but then felt she'd mishandled the call by rushing in before she'd properly explored the situation.

In discussing this call it was suggested that this may have been one of those calls where all it is possible to do is for the worker to recognise that there is a problem which the caller has to struggle with as best they can. One of the back-up social workers then gave a beautiful illustration of this point. An elderly woman with an invalid husband kept coming into the social services office asking for help. A battery of practical offers were made and rejected. One day the social worker who saw her responded to her endless complaints by saying 'I don't know how you cope'. The woman replied that he was the first person who had understood how she felt and from that time she stopped coming to the office. For once, she had felt listened to.

This point can be applied back directly to the caller's difficulty with her child. The worker had panicked because of her own anxiety (she was herself the mother of a 3 year old) and in going for an immediate practical solution had offered a random 'try everything' response which failed to contain the caller's anxiety. This is, of course, a very familiar response made by anxious parents when dealing with distressed children. Unfortunately, it serves only to increase the frustration and distress of the child thereby creating a vicious circle. It is possible that the caller was caught in this situation with her toddler, unable to bear the necessity of his frustration. Had the worker been able to offer a different response, a benign circle may have replaced the vicious one. This caller may then have become one of those who ended the call by saying 'thank you for listening, it helps to talk to someone'. This often seemed inexplicable to workers who felt they hadn't helped at all. But, as the lady said, 'listening is a useful thing'.

The value of listening is summed up by John Eldrid, the director of the Central London Branch of the Samaritans; 'I think it is essential for Samaritans to recognise that what we are offering are not solutions to problems. . .but the presence of another human being. This is a positive step towards making life more worth living' (quoted in De Le Noy, 1987). It is dreadful to feel oneself in a desperate situation from which there is no escape. This was how many, perhaps a majority, of PA's callers felt, at least at the time they called. Similarly it is painful as a worker to feel that one is powerless to help. But worse than either is to feel desperate and to cry out, yet feel that one has not been heard. Hearing the voice of desperation is the most fundamental purpose of all telephone help-lines. Only in a minority of cases are they a line to 'practical help'—in the main they are a line to the *idea* that help is possible. In other words their function is the creation and sustenance of *hope*.

When desperation has tipped over into hopelessness callers as well as workers may latch on to a request for practical help as an escape from not being able to bear to hear the reality of their situation. This is yet another variety of ambivalence—it will be recalled that the father of the glue-sniffing teenager wanted a referral to a specialist.

The following caller who was unable to resolve her ambivalence towards her husband, wanted the worker to tell her what to do.

> The woman had left her husband three times and been rehoused but had now allowed the husband to come back. She gave the worker a catalogue of the ills she suffered at her husband's hands, culminating in her fear that he was now going to throw her out of her own house.
>
> The worker suggested a court order, the council, talking to the children's school, her family, his family, the CAB. Whatever she suggested the caller could not accept. And yet she wanted to know what to do.

Clearly there was nothing she *could* do until she had been able to acknowledge the part of her that wanted/needed to stay in this desperate situation. Unable to acknowledge any of this both worker and caller lapsed into a fruitless game of 'Yes, but. . .' with the only satisfaction available to the caller being the defeat of the worker's good intentions.

The situation for PA, and indeed any help-line which offers more than a pure information service, is the reverse of that pertaining in a social service department. Rather than needing to guard against using emotional issues as a deflection of uncomfortable material demands, telephone workers need to guard against using practical information/advice as a deflection of their real purpose—the provision of a listening ear.

In order to be able to do this workers need to be able to maintain a strong conviction about the value of listening. As we have seen PA workers felt very insecure in this respect, disparaging their own resources under the impact of the feeling evoked by their callers' stories. This, in turn, tended to undermine their capacity to function as a container for the callers' anxieties.

Yet it is hardly surprising that this should have been so, given the demands they were unwittingly making on themselves. By working in their own homes as untrained volunteers they were exposing themselves to enormous stresses on maintaining a conviction in the value of their work, without having any means to minimise those stresses. (Contrast this with the Samaritans who nowadays 'severely frown' on taking calls at home and whose volunteers are never alone (De La Noy, op. cit.). One worker reported a series of calls in one evening concerned with the death of a baby, incest and a suicide. It is not easy to recover from such a bombardment—and it was not uncommon—if you are without institutional and/or professional defences. There were several occasions in the workshops when workers burst out with calls like these under the intense pressure of their need to ventilate their pent-up feelings.

Anyone who works with others in an institutional setting knows the value, the necessity, of institutional support, if only by its absence. Such support comes not only from formal channels of professional boundaries, supervision etc, but equally important from informal contact with colleagues. Letting off steam in the staff room with colleagues has enormous therapeutic potential. Denied this opportunity the worker alone in her own home has a poor choice between storing up anxieties whose level rises with each successive call or burdening a family whose tolerance and understanding may already be stretched by the repetitive intrusion of the ringing phone.

In theory, the back-ups existed to fulfil this need. But it is one thing to run into a colleague supposedly 'by the way' in the staff room or to attend a pre-arranged supervision session—it is quite another to deliberately ring someone up to say 'I need help'. Ironically, the workers found it most difficult to do what their callers were doing—confide in an anonymous stranger. All the back-ups who came to the groups found they were used much more frequently—and more for emotional support rather than merely as sources of information—once the workers had been able to put a face and familiarity on to the anonymous name and phone number. Really this is a very simple point—unless channels are provided whereby workers can offload or at least share their anxieties they are likely to become increasingly 'blocked up' and unavailable to those that need them. The provision of such channels needs to be the responsibility of the institution, not the workers themselves, so that workers feel around themselves the protection of an organisation that cares for them.

A second reason for the undermining of the workers' conviction concerns training and is therefore directly relevant to the function of the TIMS course for PA as a whole. The PA workers, like many initiates to the helping process, carried an extremely idealised image of the helping relationship. (There was some suggestion that membership of PA served to reinforce this idealisation and this issue is taken up in Chapter 4).

It was apparent from the workers distress and self-criticism when they had not responded with total sympathy and sensitivity to a caller's problem that their expectation of themselves was that they should be 'perfect counsellors'. A perfect counsellor would listen calmly and carefully, take the caller through the problem and make the 'right' response. The workers did not recognise the maelstrom of feelings evoked in them by their callers as evidence of their positive involvement with them, their willingness to allow the callers to have an impact on them, but as a failure to maintain the image of 'perfect counsellor'. This issue cropped up in the very first session—the first call presented was of a woman with whom the worker had felt extremely irritated. A lively debate ensued on this problem with a leading role being taken by one member of the group who prided herself on her 'professional' manner.

She *seemed* to epitomise what the other workers were striving for: cool, calm and collected, endlessly understanding and yet able to maintain a distance from the caller: 'I treat it as a job; I don't form an attachment.' Against this all the other workers slumped further into their feelings of inadequacy and failure for allowing themselves to be so buffeted about by their own emotions. No doubt this is a caricature of this worker's actual position but my concern here is to describe what she represented for the group.

With hindsight we saw this initial meeting as a vivid enactment by the group of the consequences of the idealised 'perfect counsellor' position with which they were burdening themselves. In fact, this sort of 'profesional manner' results in an imperviousness to the client's need: the 'perfect counsellor' denies any vulnerability in herself and pushes all the problems back into the client, creating a false polarisation, just as it occurred in the group. As the worker who spoke of her 'professional manner' put it. 'They help me a lot. I feel great because I'm not going through what they're going through—they're the one with the problem'. She was speaking of her callers but she could just as well have been speaking of the other workers. The group was enacting a mutual *fantasy* of how professionals relate to their clients. In this fantasy vulnerability is feared and devalued, yet ironically the workers capacity to be vulnerable was the very means whereby they could hope to forge an understanding with their callers. This, after all, was the point of PA—Call us, we are parents like you! They offered a shared understanding of the trials of parenthood which, at its best, amounted to an affirmation of the shared humanity of worker and caller—precisely what was excluded in their fantasy of the 'professional manner'. It was by means of what they shared with the callers that PA offered to alleviate the terrible isolation of their hopelessness and desperation. But, of course, such understanding was at the cost of irrevocably muddying the image of the 'perfect counsellor'.

To put this in professional language: The TIMS course offered to give the workers an understanding of counter-transference feelings as relevant information which could be used in the service of the client. In an oft-quoted assertion of Jung's—'You can exert no influence if you are not susceptible to influence' (Jung, 1931). But this is something which it is extremely difficult to discover on one's own. An aspiring violinist does not expect to have to learn for himself that a violin is played with a bow. He has enough work to do learning to use the bow he is given to make tuneful music. Similarly the theoretical knowledge of counter-transference does not confer on its possessors the ability to use this powerful tool skilfully but at least it relieves them from the anxiety, guilt and confusion of feeling the 'wrong' things in relation to those they are trying to help. They can at least begin the process of learning to make 'music' out of these 'wrong' feelings. The concept of being a listening ear is thus extended by an understanding of counter-transference to include listening to the worker's own responses as well as those of the help-seeker. This is the real meaning of professional detachment—far from eschewing subjectivity it requires that it be taken very seriously indeed, that it be accorded equivalent status with the so-called objective data of the external world.

Paying proper attention to counter-transference requires that the worker be in and out of the relationship at the same time. She is, ideally (!), influenced but not overwhelmed by her feelings. When these feelings are a response to what the caller/client feels about *her* (i.e. transference) it is particularly difficult to maintain this balance. However, the same principle (of maintaining balance) also applies to working with ambivalence, a central theme of PA's work as we have seen. Here the important thing is to maintain a balance between the two sides of the callers' feeling, resisting the unconscious pressure to collude in the denial of the other side. Listening to both sides, recognising that the caller is engaged in an *internal* conflict as well as the external conflict that is being ostensibly described can go a long way towards resolving ambivalence. In the call from the woman who had left her husband three times, for example, the worker was unable to hear the caller's need to stay in her unhappy marriage.

Many calls left the workers perplexed because they did not recognise the influence of inner conflict, particularly where one side of the conflict was unconscious. Callers who professed love for the children they abused could not bear to know that sometimes they wished them dead—and the PA workers too were often shocked by our suggestion that that might be the case.

> A young single mother phoned because she had shaken her six week old baby. She emphasised that she had *chosen* to have the baby against

friends' advice and therefore felt she could not now ask these friends for support.

Could it be that this lady protests too much? The emphasis on having chosen the baby might well have disguised feelings of regret—and worse, a wish to get rid of the baby (a wish represented by the friends who advised her against having it).

To 'hear' this message requires listening in a very special sense. It is listening for what is *not said*, for the unspoken language in the overt narrative. It is listening to the unconscious.

Some of the dark motives we attributed to callers, as in this case, proved difficult for the PA workers to stomach, at least initially. But it was our contention that they made sense out of what was implausible, inexplicable nonsense and could on occasion be used fruitfully to *relieve* the caller. It is perhaps asking too much of help-line workers to expect them to grasp all the intricacies of unconscious communication that psychotherapists struggle for years to master (and never really do!) But might it not have been possible for the worker to simply say to this caller 'well, of course babies are always a bit more of a handful than you expect and I suppose you sometimes wonder if you made the right decision'?

Although this would have been a simple enough comment to make, it does require some knowledge of unconscious motivations and conflicts to recognise the value of making it. It was, of course, part of our brief to develop and enchance the knowledge and skill of PA members in this way. But our training existed within the limits of the context in which they worked. An important aspect of this context was the way the workers saw their task and the way this was, in turn, influenced by their own (partly) unconscious motivations for doing it. For this reason and also because of the 'fit' between the clients' reasons for calling and the workers' reasons for being there to receive the calls it is relevant to consider the workers' personal feelings about the work in so far as they emerged in the workshops and it is with this issue that the next chapter begins.

CHAPTER FOUR

The Relationship between the Volunteers and their Callers

As Jung's dictum about being influenced suggests, the worker's own self is a most important factor in the business of helping others with their personal difficulties. This is implicit in the whole notion of 'the helping relationship' since a relationship necessarily requires that both parties are involved.

Nevertheless, it is always a tricky question to decide how far the worker's own 'personal' feelings and motives should be exposed in the service of training. At one extreme training can degenerate into personal therapy and navel-gazing or, if the recipients are less willing than their trainers, be experienced as persecutory and intrusive. At the other extreme workers may be exhorted not to become 'emotionally involved' and may end up feeling guilty when injustice and neglect makes them angry or when a client's grief brings tears to their own eyes.

In TIMS training, the general rule is to draw a boundary around those areas stimulated by the work which are purely personal and a matter for private reflection—or personal therapy—and subjective feelings which may be legitimately regarded as counter-transference information about the case under discussion. In practice, this boundary is more abstract than real (although it remains a useful reference point). Sometimes an intensely personal reminiscence may be highly relevant to the case, at other times feelings apparently evoked by the client may in truth belong to the worker. Clients may often make workers feel incompetent and confused, for example, but this is not to say that workers may not sometimes *be* incompetent and confused. Counter-transference makes a poor alibi! The fact is that nothing can be evoked unless it is already potentially there. No-one can really feel another person's feelings, although psychoanalytic ways of speaking about 'projection' and what is 'put into' workers tends to obscure this fact.

These are metaphors and like any metaphors, are done a disservice if understood literally and concretely. To use another metaphor, these processes might be understood as creating resonances, so that the client's communications, both conscious and unconscious, set up the complementary vibrations in the psyche of the worker. The skill of the worker lies in their having sufficient command over their own psychic instrument to sustain and to modify those notes which further the client's 'music' and silence those which are purely extraneous interference.

In this consideration of the worker's motivations for belonging to PA it is intended to proceed in the same way. In the loose setting of the workshops we heard a good deal about the worker's personal lives but in an unstructured, unsystematic way. We deliberately chose not to make deliberate, systematic enquiries in order to maintain the boundary described above. This does not, however, invalidate what we have to say since only what was brought into the group is relevant for our purposes *and* it is relevant because it was brought into the group. That is, what was brought into the group were those areas of the workers motivations and attitudes evoked by the work under discussion. My aim is to edit out what is 'purely' personal and focus on those elements which provide a counterpoint to the overt description of the work.

The connection between a worker's own psychic organisation and the organisation of their work setting was made several years ago by Elliot Jacques (1955) and developed by Izabel Menzies in her seminal study on nursing (Menzies, 1959). There she described the institutionalisation of certain defensive processes such as splitting and depersonalisation in the way that hospitals are organised. Nurses whose own defences mirror those of the institution are likely to feel protected by—and protective of—the organisation. Others may feel constrained and dissatisfied and would tend to leave their jobs or even the profession as a whole.

In considering the 'collective psyche' of PA I would like to focus not on the defensive processes *per se* but, borrowing a concept from marital interaction, on the dominant unconscious fantasy shared by worker and caller alike (Bannister and Pincus, 1965).

This fantasy involves an infant felt to be helpless and a parent felt to be omnipotent. Within their relationship a variety of themes are played out which may be described in terms of a triangular system made up of a persecutor, a victim and a rescuer.

The basic pattern consists of the infant in the role of victim being either persecuted or rescued by the parent, but in certain circumstances either party might take up any of the roles. The idea of a 'drama triangle' consisting of persecutor, rescuer, victim was first put forward in the context of transactional analysis (Karpman, 1968). I have found it to be an extremely valuable tool for articulating something of what goes on between mothers and their babies and within the helping relationship. Thus the PA workers provide a specific illustration of a process having much more general ramifications. It should not be thought that their tendency to get caught up in the process is in any way unique to them, far less that it implies anything but the most constructive criticism of their approach.

It is suggested that the dominance of this fantasy system coloured not only the workers' and callers' views of each other but also their attitudes to professionals, and because the fantasy remained unconscious it tended to create a limiting collusion between workers and callers in which attitudes and assumptions took on the power of 'taken for granted' reality and could not be tested. Just as in a marriage, this shared fantasy provided both a basis for understanding and a constraint on the creative responses available to both parties.

Insatiable Infants and Omnipotent Rescuers

The words most often used by PA workers in describing their feelings in relation to callers were 'helpless' and 'inadequate'. Some of the reasons for this have already been considered in terms of the intrinsic limitations of telephone work and the counter-transference feelings evoked by the callers. But what was the 'hook' in them for these counter-transference responses? Or to put it another way what assumptions of their own did the workers bring that got so stirred up by the work (i.e. what was their *transference* to their callers)?

Feelings of inadequacy do not exist in a vacuum but in relation to a presumed standard which would constitute its opposite. The workers certainly felt they were ineffective but this has to be considered in the light of what they felt was required of them.

Many of their callers phoned when they were at the extremities of emotional distress and/or were in horrendous situations. Occasionally there would be some media publicity about PA and they would then be deluged with up to 400 calls. At other times one caller would be so needy that the worker would spend up to four hours on the phone with them. Calls of one and a half to two hours were not uncommon. And such calls would frequently occur in the middle of the night. Sometimes workers would receive calls when they were not on call due to the fact that potential callers got the number of the person on call from an ansaphone and then used it at another time. Yet they were unable to refer callers back to the ansaphone. Instead they felt obliged to listen to calls *at any time* despite feeling resentful and/or flummoxed. One worker said 'you feel you are responsible. You *have* to care' and linked this feeling especially to being a woman. Another worker made a strong link between guilt and care, saying you couldn't care if you didn't feel guilty.

It was obvious to us as workshop leaders that the PA workers could not possibly meet all the demands made of them but this was not at all apparent to the workers themselves. They envisaged their callers as being in such dire need and at such desperate pitch that they could not possibly stop short of doing everything in their power to help them. Implicit in this was the idea that PA was the only port of call—that if they didn't help them nobody would. Hence when callers revealed that they were in fact in touch with other agencies this was rationalised in terms either of the other agency being no good or the caller being in some way 'false' (a hoaxer? undeserving?). When neither of these explanations sufficed the workers were often left perplexed—such situations did not fit into their stereotypical scenario.

Although in some respects their attitude to callers arose from a genuine sympathy with their plight it had in it a strong element of identification. That is, the workers tended to equate the callers with aspects of their own inner worlds, especially feelings associated with the abused child, e.g. needy and neglected on the one hand, demanding and refusing to take no for an answer on the other. (In psychoanalytic theory this process, whereby aspects of the self are attributed to another who is then regarded as the embodiment of those aspects, is known as projective identification). Even allowing for the power of the callers' feelings to evoke a desired response, the fact that the workers so frequently fell into this kind of helpless, limitless attitude suggests that the work was activating something in *them* which, in turn, was getting projected into the callers, so that, in the end, it would be hard to say whether they were reacting to the caller or to their own projections. These workers had, after all, chosen to work for an agency whose avowed task was to save the abused child. The image of the abused child in need of rescue must therefore have been a powerfully charged one in their minds. But unlike, say, the NSPCC which concentrates on the child directly, PA aimed to reach the child through the potentially abusing parents. The need for PA arose from a recognition of the cycle of deprivation—i.e. that it is the abused child who becomes the abusing parent. There was therefore an ambiguity in their approach to callers—a dilemma admittedly shared by many in the child care field—as to whether they were 'child centred' or 'parent centred'. The predominant impression left by their attitude and response to callers was that 'parent and child' had become conflated in their minds. It was as though the callers had become the infants and the workers had become the parents compelled by guilt, care and responsibility to meet their insatiable demands. But if the demands were insatiable, the workers would have to be omnipotent in order to meet them. Indeed, the more outrageous the demands the more the workers found themselves seduced into an omnipotent fantasy of what could be done.

During the crisis provoked by the multi-hoax fantasy caller discussed in Chapter 2 (p 26–27), while what seemed like half of PA was running around trying to 'save' this supposed child one worker attempted to refer her to the Tavistock Clinic. A bemused but very experienced secretary upon hearing the situation replied 'What am I supposed to do?' This response seemed not to have occurred in to anyone in PA.

The point I am making here will be recognised as the obverse of the point made in relation to the callers in Chapter 2. There I described this self-same dynamic, whereby the callers became the infants and the workers the parents, in terms of counter-transference—i.e. the result of the callers' unconscious pressure on the workers to feel and react in a certain way. Now I am suggesting that this was a two-way process—that there was a 'fit' between workers and callers such that the workers were as ready to see the callers as insatiable infants as the callers were to see them anonymous parents. This is what is meant by saying that both parties were dominated by a shared unconscious fantasy.

It will also be seen that in making this point I am transgressing the usual boundary in which workers' own feelings are left private. I would say, however, that these were not matters that were directly spoken of in the workshops and they are dealt with here only for the purpose of indicating the complex dynamics aroused by this kind of work. In the practice of training the personal aspect can normally be addressed implicitly through the work since, so long as the workers are reasonably in touch with reality, it is the work itself which arouses the more personal dimension.

It would be worth looking more closely at the omnipotent rescuer/insatiable infant dynamic as it is relevant not only to the motivations of the PA worker (and no doubt others in the child care field) but to the dynamics of child abuse itself.

None of the PA workers spoke directly of having been abused children themselves and only one or two admitted having been abusing parents. It will be remembered that this was not a criterion for membership of PA. Workers had only to be parents themselves, parents who *understood* the difficulties of potentially abusing parents. Yet how could they understand unless they shared a little of the same experience? The PA ethos was that the abusing parent is only at the extreme end of a continuum—a difference of degree rather than kind. Hence their difficulties with incest callers, who, as has been suggested, were experienced as different in kind.

All of us will have experienced some neglect or abuse as children by virtue of the fact that neither parents nor children are perfect. Parents cannot be endlessly available to children and children cannot always tolerate this. There is frustration and disappointment, and sometimes grief and rage, on both sides. All of this gives body to an image of the child-in-need which I believe to be archetypal, i.e. an inherent potential for a complex of feelings, experiences and ideas. But this complex contains not only the passive hurts of the victim but also the active wish for transcendence: the mobilisation of aggression into the strength and power required to put right what was felt to be wrong.

In *Macbeth*, Shakespeare uses the figure of the infant as a combined image of outraged innocence and the call for justice:

> And Pity, like a naked new-born babe
> Striding the blast, or heaven's Cherubins, hors'd
> Upon the sightless couriers of the air
> Shall blow the horried deed in every eye
> That tears shall drown the wind (Act I sc.vii ll.21–25)

In this image the infant, far from being helpless and impotent, is a figure of great force and power. And this corresponds not only to what psychoanalysis suggests about the feelings of infants themselves but to the experience of parents in response to their children.

It is a biological necessity that when the infant cries the mother feels an instinctual demand to respond to its needs. As Bowlby and Winnicott have stressed, the mother/infant relationship is a reciprocal one. I would add to this that no small part of the mother's response is through the activation of the needy child within herself. She is in a state of identification with her infant (hardly surprising since the real infant has literally been inside her) and this experience of herself-as-infant functions like an antenna through which the infant's needs are transmitted. Messages that are transmitted through a medium, however, are liable to the distortions imposed by that medium. The way she will receive her infant's demands depends how she herself was treated as a child. If she felt that her experience was at the good end of the continuum she will feel that she has enough resources (more or less) to satisfy her infant. If she was approximately at the middle her needy child may function as a rescuer: She responds to a sense that her infant is in acute pain and seeks to rescue her, thereby enacting the child's wish for the required strength and power to right the wrongs done to her. Depending on all the vagaries of the mother/child fit and the nature of the environment in which all this takes place, the child may become either a source of reassuring joy or of anxious disappointment, thus setting the scene for the next generational act. But towards the 'bad' end of the continuum the child within may rise up like an avenger turning on the less than perfect parent she now is, demanding perfection and threatening retribution against the sins of generations past. Such a parent feels an internal demand for perfection against an ever present threat of persecution if this is not achieved. Only omnipotence can protect her from the abuse she herself suffered and, most crucially, fears she may now suffer at the hands of her infant. We are back to Shakespeare's paradox of the power of the helpless infant. The torment of the internal persecution is experienced as though it were coming from without—the medium has become confused with the message. In extreme cases, real physical abuse may result from acts of retaliation against such an avenging inner voice, like some kind of horribly involuted vendetta.

The PA workers saw themselves as rescuers but the environment in which they were working was not conducive to the satisfaction of their own internal needs, in that telephone work is so inherently frustrating. One might then ask 'Why on earth do they do it?' but the irony is that *only* people with a wish/need to try and be omnipotent would take on such a job. Since omnipotent fantasies are a compensation for feelings of helplessness it makes sense that only people who felt a strong identification with the abused/needy child and were aroused to act as rescuers, yet felt themselves to be of little value and to have little to offer would opt for such an unpaid, ungratifying form of offering help. On this level the workers' frequently expressed feelings of inadequacy said more about how they felt about themselves and their work than it said about their actual performance. (Bearing in mind their belief that their attitudes were associated with their being women, it is also a poor comment on the value and status society offers to women in general and mothers in particular).

This point has implications for both volunteers and professionals in so far as these motives are common to both. But professional training does at least confer some sense of status and value as well as containing a de-idealising component—the image of the 'hard-bitten professional' is the very antithesis of omnipotence: whether policeman, journalist or social worker he is always presented in countless TV series, films and books as a disappointed idealist, both vulnerable and tough, carrying on a lengthy crusade which he knows he can never win against the forces of power, corruption and stupidity.

Professionals are socialised both through their training and their subsequent membership of the professional group into a set of values attitudes and structures (ways of doing things) which restrain omnipotent fantasies by setting boundaries to the expectations of worker and client alike. Clearly such containment is not always sufficient since many professional carers are also exposed to impossible demands through work overload, lack of organisational support, positive interference from the organisation (e.g. health service administrators versus consultants or local councillors versus social workers) or, particularly in the case of social workers, contradictory public expectations. These are the kind of circumstances leading to the well-known 'burn-out' syndrome which essentially results from a sense of there being an unmanageable gulf between personal expectations, ideals etc. and actual achievement. It should be clear that the omnipotent/impotent polarity is thus a critical factor in burn-out.

Volunteers, (and voluntary agencies staffed by paid by non-professional staff) are free of many of the constraints of professionals but this is a two-edged sword: on the one hand they bring to the job a sense of inspiration and enthusiasm which is open to new ways of thinking and working, because untrammelled by professional socialisation; on the other they are directly exposed to client need and demand without the protection of professional boundaries to keep them on the well-trodden path.

In this kind of environment omnipotent fantasies may be positively fostered as part of the inspirational ideology, but at what cost to the workers and ultimately the agency itself? My own first social work job was in a voluntary agency which ran an open-door day centre for drug addicts. We fully believed in the valuable therapeutic work we were doing despite the fact that addicts were literally dying in front of our eyes. I was stung when the Chairman of the management committee, a consultant psychiatrist, suggested that the project was actually fulfilling no more than a basic humanitarian function akin to a soup-kitchen, but that it was necessary for the workers to believe that it was more than that to make working there tolerable. In fact, workers did realise fairly quickly the true situation: the burn-out rate was high and there was a correspondingly high turnover of staff.

There was some suggestion that PA was facing a similar collective crisis at the point when they first made contact with us. We heard faint rumblings of dissatisfaction with the organisation and certainly there was a strong feeling that they were not equipped for the task they were expected to do, hence the wish for training. One function of the workshops was therefore to provide essential protection and support akin to that provided by professional socialisation but not so identical with it as to destroy the original inspirational character of the agency. This issue is taken up again and considered in more detail in the next chapter on Professionalisation and the final chapter on Parents Anonymous in Context.

The lack of boundaries made the PA workers particularly vulnerable on three counts—identification, collusion and persecution. Each of these will be discussed in turn.

Identification

One of the crucial differences between professionals and the PA workers concerned the relative absence amongst the PA workers of a sense of distance between themselves and their clients. Again there is an irony here in that the telephone provided an in-built physical and geographical distance and it is plausible that it was because of their difficulty in maintaining emotional distance that the workers opted to volunteer for a telephone helpline which provided them with some safeguards. Often workers would want to rush round and help their callers cope but this was rarely practicable and the befriending service seemed little used. The notable exception to this approach was provided by the worker who said 'I treat it as a job' and 'I'm not the one with the problem' (p 42). This distorted version of a professional attitude underlined both the positive and negative aspects of the other workers' contrasting stance of *identification* with their callers. Although they avoided becoming detached and remote the other workers frequently ended up in exactly the opposite position, feeling 'I *am* the one with the problem'.

Although identification can be useful as a way of getting in touch with others, it requires the capacity to discriminate between one's own problem and that of the other. Failure to do so results in the helper feeling burdened by responsibility for a problem they feel unable to leave alone, and the helped feeling un-helped, because the helper is not properly in tune with *them*. One PA worker spoke of spending all day on the phone for a caller: 'Suddenly you realise it's become more important to you than it is to them or else you've frightened them away. Sometimes I think they just say yes to keep you happy'.

The sense of identification, particularly when it was not recognised, produced a feeling of *having* to help the caller and led to enormous anxiety if this was not possible. This can be understood in terms of the need to prevent the victim-child with whom the worker identified from turning into the persecutor-child who threatened dire punishment if perfect solutions were not found for all problems.

An alternative scenario would be to blame the 'child' caller for their failure to accept the help offered—the rescuer turning into a persecutor. Thus one worker who was quite explicit about her personal motives for joining PA said that she sometimes found relying on her own experience a disadvantage since she became impatient with callers who did not respond to the solutions that had worked for her. A third danger of identification was that the caller's problem itself would feel like a reproach: for example, the worker who found herself unable to really listen to a caller whose three-year-old son was having enormous tantrums because of anxiety about her mothering of her own three-year-old boy (p 39).

Collusion

When two or more people share an unconscious fantasy they are likely to create a relationship in which the fantasy is enacted as if it were reality. Their unconscious 'agreement' to do so may be described as *collusion.* Each partner has their assigned role which they can be induced to play out by a variety of subtle cues (Laing 1969).

The PA workers' wish to live up to an image of an omnipotent rescuer laid them wide open to colluding with some of their callers' insatiable demands. Indeed in some respects they fostered collusion themselves. The original posters advertising PA said 'Don't hurt your child. Call us'. But these were changed in 1984, leaving out direct reference to child abuse and instead emphasising parents under stress. The policy behind this was to spread their net wider in the hope of operating a more preventative service. However, it could be argued that in so doing they were inviting more demand than they could possibly meet, deliberately abrogating what few boundaries they possessed. There may also have been a defensive aspect to the change, inspired by a possibly unconscious wish to dilute the unrelieved diet of child abuse calls. Interestingly, a similar development occurred at Childline which, only a few months after its inception, began presenting itself as for *all* children—even though it had been notoriously difficult to get through to when targeted only at child abuse.

These changes of emphasis towards providing a universal service service, to *all* parents or *all* children, are closely analogous to the reorganisation in 1971 of local authority social services into mammoth unified departments following the recommendations of the Seebohm committee. There appeared to be an excellent rationale for the change: the need to prevent the duplication of services which resulted from having separate departments for health, child care, welfare, mental health etc. It was hoped to provide a more unified and flexible service but it was also explicitly intended to be a *universal* service, abolishing once and for all the stigma associated with 'the welfare'. This was undoubtedly a noble intention but with hindsight it has become clear that its realisation depends upon the availability of virtually unlimited resources. However desirable, this is never likely to be the case and the need for some rationing is inevitable.

PA workers felt they had to provide a resource which offered to cure all and was endlessly available—and that resource could only be themselves. Their inability to say no to callers led them into ironic situations of exploitation and abuse. They became the victims of their own—and their callers omnipotent fantasies. One of the commonest problems faced by workers was how to 'wind down' calls and also how to deal with callers who rang incessantly at inconvenient times. A classic example of this sort of difficulty was reported by a worker who took a call at 1.30 a.m. which went on for an hour. The telephone was in the hall and for the entire duration of the call she stood shivering in her nightie, unable even to ask the caller to hold on while she got a dressing gown! In the work with incest and fantasy callers the tendency to collusion had more serious consequences since it fostered their callers fantasies of unlimited gratification. Furthermore the workers had to suffer the abuse of hearing graphic details of sexual perversion or psychotic fantasies.

Persecution

Up to a point it could be said that workers allowed themselves to be exploited because it satisfied their unconscious need to see themselves as omnipotent rescuers—despite the irony that the more they identified with this fantasy the more they became victims of the callers' abuse. But some callers deliberately (albeit perhaps unconsciously) manipulated the workers' vulnerability by playing on their need to rescue. One incest caller succeeded in keeping the worker on the phone by telling her that talking to him was the only thing stopping him from abusing his daughter. Only after several such calls did the worker cotton on to what a 'sucker' she was being. Of course, this caller was using exactly the kind of blackmail that sexual abusers use to get children to keep their mouths shut about what is happening to them.

In the scenario where callers used their 'victim' status to coerce the worker into listening to them the roles were effectively reversed: the so-called victim became the persecutor and the ostensible rescuer the victim. This was especially true of the fantasy callers who almost always presented themselves as helpless victims of horrendous abuse. These callers activated the workers' fear of being attacked from within by the avenging child if they did not provide the help demanded of them. Caught between the devil and the deep blue sea they were, instead, attacked from without by the persecuting victim. Thus do the abused become abusers in their turn, biting the hand that seeks to feed them.

The Fantasy of the Omnipotent Rescuer

At the root of the fantasy of the omnipotent rescuer lies the magical belief that all damage can be eradicated, all wounds healed, all losses made good. Ironically, the more energy is invested in this belief, the less it is available for real activity in the world. Thus the more PA colluded with their callers, the less they were actually able to help them and the more inadequate they felt. But their 'inadequacy' needs to be recognised as a failure to meet their own—and their callers'—perfectionistic standards, a failure for which they felt themselves to be perpetually at risk of persecution.

All this has a very familiar ring to it. It is surely no coincidence that social workers find themselves the targets of just such persecution for their failure to eradicate child abuse. Notwithstanding the public policy issues raised by a succession of child abuse deaths, the abuse and persecution of social workers in their wake has all the landmarks of the victim who persecutes the rescuer for their failure to solve all problems. Especially in a social climate where deprivation is increasing along with social division between haves and have nots and there is anxiety about whether future resources will be sufficient to meet growing needs, it is perhaps to be expected that the archetypal child-in-need is making his presence felt in the collective psyche, as a persecuting avenger.

Accordingly, the fantasy of the omnipotent rescuer is also deeply pervasive in the truly fantastic expectations that are publicly placed on social workers. As previously mentioned the seeds of this are to be found in the post-war welfare ideology of *universalism* which led to the creation of mammoth social service departments with cradle to the grave responsibilities. The relatively rapid creation of an affluent society in the West out of the devastation of post-war ruins provided apparent material support for omnipotent illusions which flowered so attractively, yet so briefly, in the 1960s, and the Seebohm Committee's report in 1971 should be seen in this context. As the economic climate has changed and the political climate along with it, expectations of social welfare have shifted away from hope and benevolence toward pessimism and persecution.

The omnipotent rescuer fantasy seeks to obliterate all frustration and aggression, not to say persecution, since aggression, (which has a creative as well as a destructive aspect), is the response to unmet need. This wish can be clearly discerned in the so-called flower-power ethos of the 1960s. Yet it is a paradoxical wish in that it is only through the mobilisation of aggression as assertion and determination that unmet need can be overcome.

When aggression is not recognised and given its due as in the collusion of rescuer/victim it is bound to return as the threat of persecution. Perhaps it would be more accurate to describe the rescuer/victim collusion as a defence against underlying persecution anxiety—the fear that aggressive feelings will be overwhelming and destructive. In this collusion there is always a dilemma: what to do with the persecutor. By implication the persecutor is always elsewhere—the abusing other. But this only allows him to creep into the interaction via the back door. PA workers generally took up a 'masochistic' position whereby as we have seen, they allowed themselves to be exploited by the persecutor-in-the-victim.

There is also the alternative danger of a 'sadistic' helping position where the worker is taken over, in whole or in part, by an identification with the persecutor. The caricature of the snooping social worker is an example of this, none the less illustrative for being a media stereotype. Just as social workers do try to be the omnipotent rescuers that the 'public' (i.e. the media) expects, so they may fall prey to a persecutory attitude towards their clients.

A more complex, and potentially serious example of this is the recent wave of concern over sexual abuse. Pioneering professionals in this field have testified to the way they are treated like the 'victims'—i.e. disbelieved, blamed, persecuted etc. However the question must also be asked whether they are not also in danger of taking on the features of the persecutor by virtue of their identification with an omnipotent crusading position. It is unlikely, to say the least, that a human experience as basic and primitive as incest, and as common to all cultures, can ever be stamped out. Too much moral fervour in the attempt is likely to produce the counter-productive effect described by Bob Dylan in his satirical comment on American liberals who 'don't hate nothing at all except hatred' (Dylan, 1965). However difficult it is to draw in practice, there is a line between investigation and intrusion and between raising public awareness and abuse of social propriety. Is it really only because of denial that people do not want to hear about sexual abuse? May there not also be a sense that the taboo can be broken not only in actions but also in the too graphic nature of words spoken about it? All this may have enormous positive value for those children who can be 'rescued' but my point is to draw attention to the 'shadow' side of the rescuer, namely, the persecutor.

It is perhaps only to be expected that in a field such as child sexual abuse everyone ends up feeling persecuted by everyone else. The tragedy of Cleveland (Butler-Sloss, 1988) is not that the professionals were incompetent, far less uncaring, but that they were overwhelmed by the perversity of the situations with which they were confronted. They must have been blinded by the same righteous indignation they aroused in those they subsequently wrongly accused. Could it be that the feelings aroused in the doctors and social workers were so unbearable that they were unable to contain them and instead used the 'innocents' as the 'victims' of their projections as a way of attempting to get rid of feelings of corruption and damage which, as actual incest survivors testfiy, are almost impossible to eradicate? Thus, once more, do the abused become abusers in their turn.

The more omnipotent a rescuer becomes, the more he is at risk of being taken over by the persecutory aspect of his activities. The most extreme and therefore dramatically vivid form of this kind of moral panic is the Inquisition, where would-be rescuers of souls took up the most ferociously sadistic positions, in relation to supposed victims of the Devil (Umberto Eco's *Name of the Rose* (1983) provides a detailed reconstruction of the kind of thinking involved, emphasising the messianic belief in possession of the Truth).

Well beyond the middle ages Western history is littered with similar examples of collective hysteria in the form of witch-hunts. Indeed, what more apposite image could there be for the embodiment of unconscious feelings about cruelty to children than that of the bad-witch mother of fairy tales such as Hansel and Gretel, Sleeping Beauty and Rapunzel?

The helping relationship must always contain a large element of victim and rescuer or, in less stark terms, of wounded and healer (Groesbeck 1975). But if it is to be truly effective it must also find a place for the *wounder* (Curry 1984), the representation of inevitable pain, conflict and even hate, in any loving relationship. Seen in this light persecution is a distortion of the proper use of aggressive energies in the service of transcending the position of the helpless child-victim. Conversely the collusion to exclude those energies results in a serious depletion of the possibilities available within a helping relationship, especially the opportunity for *confrontation*.

Setting firm limits and boundaries requires the workers to assert themselves—there is a cruelty in saying to a distressed person 'I can't speak to you any longer now'. These areas form one axis of the skills which we helped the PA workers develop over the course of the workshop—the assertive axis. The other axis was concerned with listening and containment—the nurturing axis. The next chapter describes the application of these skills in more detail and the resulting modification of the workers oscillation between omnipotence and impotence.

CHAPTER FIVE

The Professionalisation of PA

In the course of our work with PA it became increasingly apparent that we were dealing with an agency in crisis. Demands were being made on it that not only outstripped its capacity to respond but also required a shift in its basic ethos. In as much as PA had been set up by parents for parents it was imbued with the ethos of a self-help group. The workers' identification with many of their callers was in accord with a self-help approach since mutual identification forms both the basis on which self-help groups are founded and the therapeutic agent by which they work. However, as we have seen, for PA identification was fraught with pitfalls and in many cases was inappropriate or inadequate to meet their callers needs.

The ethos of self-help eschews expertise and values informality, ease of access and a deliberate absence of boundaries between helper and helped. The language of client and worker is foreign to it—all are members. Depending on their task their *modus vivendi* is either 'I've been there and come through it so you can too' or 'we're in this together, let's solve it together'. Alcoholics Anonymous is the example par excellence of the first kind and its name alone shows the debt which PA owes to AA; examples of the second kind range from groups which come together to work on a defined task, such as a group of mothers setting up crèche and playgroup facilities, to mutual support and information groups such as those which exist for a variety of mental and physical disabilities. An example close to home for PA is Crysis, a national network of support groups for parents of crying babies, to which PA workers sometimes made referrals. Such groups may also act as pressure groups on behalf of their members.

A brief consideration of how such groups fulfil a therapeutic function for their members will illustrate how different they actually are from PA. Primarily they are *groups* and rely on group phenomena for their effectiveness. AA combines a judicious mixture of group pressure and group support. Other groups of the second kind may offer support alone, since they are not necessarily concerned with altering destructive addictive behaviour.

In some cases those who form or join a self-help group find that the sense of purpose provided by the group becomes itself a way of dealing with the original problem. This can have a benign aspect in that those who are suffering from loss or disability of some kind may find a way to turn their suffering to creative account on behalf of others. An impressive but by no means exceptional example is Diana Lamplugh whose daughter Suzy was apparently abducted by a client while working as an estate agent and has since disappeared without trace. Mrs Lamplugh has now founded the Suzy Lamplugh Trust which aims to promote self-awareness and self-protection amongst women at work.

Finally, self-help groups may utilise the familiar group process of uniting against a common enemy. To some extent this is the case with all pressure groups but it is particularly true of numerous religious and political organisations where the salvation of those within is predicated on the damnation of those without. I have, for example, heard it said by Marxist critics of psychoanalysis that the Russian Revolution cured more neuroses than Freud ever did. While this may have been true for a number of Bolsheviks, one has only to look at the subsequent 'side-effects' to seriously question the validity of such a 'cure'.

Although some of these functions may have been fulfilled for some of the workers, PA did not exist primarily to help its volunteers. Thus, although it espoused the self-help ethos, this could not properly be maintained since there was a very real division between the volunteers and the callers. For the callers there *was* no group, only the one-to-one relationship, with the anonymous parent at the other end of the phone. PA could offer support or even pressure to help parents stop abusing their children but without the amplified power that is created by the group process. Some of the smaller Parents Anonymous groups outside London are able to create more overlap between volunteers and callers by offering support groups and crèche facilities (e.g. PALS, based in Welwyn). But in an enormous metropolis like London this is clearly virtually impossible.

The possibilities for the therapeutic use of identification are further limited by the distance which is a given of the anonymous telephone call. Apart from its other limitations, in the absence of support groups it reduces the likelihood of any cross-over from the role of the helped to that of the helper almost to nil. Some of the people who turned up asking to be volunteers may really have been disguising their need for help, but those who phoned for help had already made clear which side of the fence they wanted to be on.

Nor could the PA workers invoke the AA 'I've-been-there-too' approach since they had not usually been abusers themselves. Instead they attempted to modify the formula to 'I'm like you so I can understand'. However, as has been amply illustrated, they were frequently confronted by situations quite beyond their own experience and in these cases, particularly those concerned with incest, their feeling was more like 'I'm *not* like you and I *don't* understand'. These cases not only increased the distance between worker and caller, but also, more acutely, they increased the *need* for the workers to distance themselves for their own emotional survival.

Several workers expressed their awareness of these difficulties by saying 'Our callers now expect us to provide a *service*'. At first this statement struck us as a little odd—what else would they be expecting? But in the light of the above considerations it is apparent that the workers had previously assumed a we're-all-in-it-together ideology and only now were coming to see themselves as one group of people (volunteer workers) providing a service for another group of people (callers or, dare it be said, clients).

The enthusiasm and commitment which they had brought to the work now seemed inadequate—'love is not enough'. If they were going to provide a service they needed the proper skills and it was out of this need that the request for training was made to the TIMS.

But this request was no simple matter. It will be recalled that there was uncertainty almost up to the starting date about whether the first group would run. On the other hand the second workshop was so oversubscribed that we had to offer two groups. And, even then, there were some PA members who, apparently, looked askance at what the workshop was doing. All this indicates that there was considerable ambivalence towards change within the organisation. The move away from the self-help ethos towards 'providing a service' involved the organisation in a crisis of purpose and direction that revolved around its stance *vis-à-vis* professional agencies.

This was a question which also exercised us—how much did we as professional workers have to offer to untrained volunteers? We felt like anthropologists or missionaries going into unknown territory, feeling we had something of value to offer but anxious lest our involvement destroyed the very culture to which we were offering it. Nevertheless in some ways the TIMS was an appropriate choice since we too are a 'voluntary' agency, i.e. not part of the statutory services.

Neither the TIMS nor the PA workers wanted us to turn them into professionals, yet we came to feel that they did need to become more professional. This apparent paradox rests in part on a semantic confusion but the semantic confusion also indicates the substantive problem.

The term professional is, of course, used in two different ways. In one sense, usually as an adjective, it means properly competent and qualified—this is the sense in which PA needed to become more professional in order to provide the service required of it. In its other sense, usually as a noun, it refers to a member of a profession, a defined group of people with set requirements for training and admission to membership, agreed tasks and standards of practice and self-imposed sanctions. Professionals are also distinguished from volunteers in some contexts and amateurs in others in that they are paid for what they do. There is, however, the additional confusion that an agency like the TIMS staffed by well-trained paid professionals, is nevertheless called a voluntary agency in that it is not part of the statutory services.

The substantive problem reflected in the sematic overlap is that what would make the PA workers more professional—and what they clearly needed—was some degree of psychological knowledge over and above their own experience and the ability to set appropriate boundaries as to whom they helped, how they helped them and the nature of the relationship between them. Yet these two areas—knowledge/expertise and boundary setting are also what defines the activities of professions, apart from their membership of professional organisations and the fact that they are paid. Was this really what they wanted if they were to remain an *alternative* to the professional services? This whole issue was deeply coloured by their *attitude* to professionals. But before looking at this I want to stay with the substantive problem of what sort of agency a voluntary help-line is or should be if it is not a self-help group.

Towards the end of the workshop after a number of shifts had occurred in the direction of professionalisation one worker expressed the problem in terms of a forceful defence of her own intuitive approach. 'We are *not* counsellors,' she said. 'You have to go from your guts.' She contrasted this with professionals who have to have objectivity and be at one remove from the experience. And to the back-ups and me she said: 'I don't know how you social workers do it'. This put the dilemma in a nutshell in that it cut both ways—the statement 'we are *not* counsellors' could be seen as an appropriate statement of boundaries and difference but could act as a block against learning and the development of skill. The distinction between the volunteer's 'guts' and the professional's 'objectivity' epitomises the fear that these are mutually opposed and that professional skill will be at the expense of feeling and spontaneity. There is an analogy in the attitude of some jazz musicians who hesitate to learn to read music, fearing that their inspiration would be imprisoned by the rows of black dots. Yet those rows of black dots can open up whole vistas of music that even the sharpest ear could not master without them.

It was actually through relying too exclusively on their guts that the PA workers had fallen prey to omnipotence since, in the absence of institutional boundaries, their sympathy for their callers and their strong urge to help had led them into taking on all comers. Although, as the table of calls showed, there was almost always a parent-child problem somewhere there were many calls where it was not the direct focus and/or where it was merely a hook to hang the caller's problem on. It was inevitable that with such an indiscriminate response the workers would frequently find themselves unable to help and would then swing to the alternate pole of feeling impotent and useless.

Taking the problem of what was or was not an appropriate call from a somewhat different perspective, we wondered whether the widening of PA's focus to the point where it threatened to have no focus at all served as an *avoidance* of their primary function, namely to respond to child abuse. On this view, the omnipotence of taking on all and sundry constituted a defence against the painful feelings of inadequacy and impotence stirred up by the horror of the abuse calls. If so it was a singularly unsuccessful defence since the barrage of callers presenting problems with which PA did not feel equipped to cope only served to exacerbate their feelings of uselessness.

Setting Limits

This whole issue was brought to a head by the multi-hoax caller who claimed to be a 12/13 year old American girl in a kaleidoscopic variety of horrendous situations (Chapter 2, p 26). The coming together of the two groups to discuss this caller acted as a watershed after which PA as a whole (in the shape of its Executive Committee) woke up to the urgent need to produce some organisational guidelines which would begin to set boundaries to this type of exploitation. It will be remembered that the PA response which had allowed this very disturbed caller to invade the entire workshop was in sharp contrast to how we learnt that the Samaritans had dealt with her—by issuing instructions that volunteers were not to take calls from her. PA simply lacked the structure to do this, since apart from the workshop there was no way of closely monitoring incoming calls.

Our leadership of the group played an important role in enabling the PA committee (a number of whose members were in the workshop) to assert some authority. We were clearly role models for them, despite the obvious differences between us. In the first workshop members had explicitly valued the structure, commitment and informed professional input as well as eulogising us as 'absolutely fantastic listeners'. Towards the end of this double-group meeting we had done what the PA workers were unable to do: asserted our own authority and called a halt to the discussion of this bizarre and troublesome caller. Although we later heard that this caused some disgruntlement among the members and that, significantly, they felt we were distancing ourselves from them, it acted as a strong incentive for them to take action themselves.

A few weeks after the 'double group' the PA committee issued a number of guidelines. Third party calls were not to be accepted and ongoing calls had to be brought to the Committee after a certain length of time to prevent workers becoming too embroiled. The Committee would then decide whether or not it was appropriate for the calls to continue. Workers were also required to attend at least one out of every four support groups. This was thought to be necessary both for the worker's benefit and also as a way for the agency to monitor what individual workers were up to.

These modest proposals represented an important shift in PA's thinking. They recognised that workers should *not* accept all comers and included some notion that the work needs to be monitored. In addition to these guidelines, workers in the groups recognised the need for boundaries concerning the length and frequency of calls and began to assert their right not to take calls at any time of the day or night when they were not on duty.

Although these limits generally restricted access to the workers and were therefore a move away from a self-help ethos in the direction of a more professional approach, setting limits could also serve to differentiate between the tasks and areas of competence appropriate to PA and those appropriate to a professional agency. In the following call the worker was able to correctly assess her own potential contribution and refer the caller for further help.

> A woman rang about the conflict between her son from her first marriage and her second husband. The step-father appeared to be jealous of the boy and the boy was disruptive and obstreperous. She and her husband could not agree about him. What should she do? The worker suggested family therapy via a referral from GP or health clinic.

In presenting the call the worker wondered whether she should have gone further into the dynamics of the situation with the caller—e.g. explored the notion that the son's difficulties were an expression of the family conflicts. However, another worker (who had been instrumental in drawing up the new guidelines) thought not: 'We would be taking on more than we are qualified for, leading callers up the garden path and opening doors where we are not able to follow through'.

This view of the matter recognises that PA's appropriate task may be to provide a first step towards help by enabling callers to recognise the need for help but that it cannot itself provide that help. Although this appears to severely limit its function it is actually to relieve the workers of the hopeless struggle to be omnipotent and to allow them to do what they do best and what most callers expected of them—to provide a listening ear.

Some workers were keen to develop their skills by gaining more psychological knowledge, or were in any event plain interested. To some extent we agreed that this was necessary and the workshops provided a good deal of psychological interpretation of callers' situations. However, by the end of the workshops we felt that this too was an area where limits needed to be set. However valuable a greater 'knowledge base' might be to the workers as individuals we were not sure it would help them do their job—and it could even hinder them by encouraging them to get out of their depth (a little knowledge, as the saying goes, can be a dangerous thing). This seemed to be one of the annoyances with us after the 'double-group'—that we had rejected any attempt to *understand* the caller and instead focused on what to do about her. The same attitude characterised our attitude to the incest callers. Our position was that while some knowledge was necessary to sensitise workers to the nuances of situations and enable them to respond appropriately, their task was not to provide telephone therapy—it is dubious whether such a thing really exists—but truly to be a helpline—i.e. a line to help. In that sense the worker who said 'We are not counsellors' was spot on. Where the workers could use their own ordinary experience and understanding they could be directly helpful to callers within the confines of their limited task. The support and reassurance they provided to mothers at the end of their tethers was the best example of this as well as being what the agency was originally set up to do. When callers presented problems that were outside their ordinary experience they needed not so much knowledge of psychology as an awareness of appropriate boundaries.

The purpose of the training we provided was to enable them to do what they did best better. Thus we strove to help them improve the quality of their listening by developing their capacity to attend to unconscious cues. On the other hand the workshops developed their capacity not only to be aware of boundaries but also to have the confidence to enforce them. In practice this could mean either refusing to listen to callers, referring them on or limiting the availability of the listening ear they provided.

In a sense this made them more 'professional' but without destroying that aspect of their essential function which was to provide an alternative to the professional network of services. This requirement could only be fulfilled by ordinary volunteers, with no special qualifications, able to make a direct link with their anonymous callers. To this extent the sense of identification between worker and caller remained important, though in a different context. Perhaps it would be more accurate to say that whereas previously there had existed an unconscious assumption that worker and caller were identical, there was now the possibility that recognition of similarities *and* differences could be used to foster a relationship, however brief, of mutual respect and reciprocity.

Chad Varah, in setting up the Samaritans, seems to have been very aware of this need to provide an alternative to professional services while doing so in a 'professional' way. In *Samaritans in the '70s* (1973) he describes how he wanted the Samaritans to be 'the best friend anyone ever had in a desperate situation' and yet, in another passage, describes them as people who, although not doctors, were still professionals. The distinction is best summed up in his account of the situation which existed before the Samaritans come into being:

> There were plenty of hospitals and doctors, caseworkers and clergy, all of them offering some kind of specialist help, but it was difficult for a lonely, anxious or depressed person to find someone trustworthy to unburden to and talk things over with *before making up his/her mind whether expert help was needed and acceptable or not* (italics added)

In order to provide such a service Varah realised that it was necessary for the agency to have clear aims, namely a reduction in the numbers of suicides, *not* any general reduction of human misery. He also mentions that he came to realise that some people were unhelpable. The point about limits of this sort is that it is the exclusion of that which is beyond the boundaries which enables effective work to be done within them. This point was previously made in relation to *Yosser's Story*, where Yosser's demand for instant help prevented his psychiatrist from helping another patient. But it is now possible to see that it is not necessary or desirable that PA should have *no* boundaries so that they can be available to the Yossers of this world but that their boundaries are different to those of professional agencies. Football and tennis are very different games but without a bounded space within which the game takes place neither would be possible.

Attitudes to Professionals—Suckers or Bastards

I want to approach the PA workers' attitudes to professionals by way of a comparison with the attitudes to social workers of some clients in a social service department as described by Mattinson and Sinclair (1979) in *Mate and Stalemate*. These intensely ambivalent clients tended to see the world as a hostile place filled with persecutors. When faced by their often outrageous but very insistent demands, social workers experienced a strong pull to either enact—and thereby confirm—the client's scenario by becoming the 'bastards' that withhold resources/ help or to invert the scenario by giving in and becoming the 'sucker' to the client's manipulation. The client seeks a rescuer and the worker to rescue but hostility, ambivalence and prior expectations collapse the triangle into a two dimensional tug of war: there are only two roles available in the client's inner world and the workers have to struggle hard indeed to resist colluding with either position.

Although it is not spelled out by Mattinson and Sinclair the opposition between suckers and bastards is closely tied up with the setting of appropriate boundaries. Under the intense pressure of client need and the anger, anxiety and frustration which stem from their inability to meet it, public service agencies frequently feel it necessary to tighten their boundaries and create a thicker and more rigid distance between themselves and their clients. Such a boundary is concretised in the plate-glass screens that have for a long time separated clerk and claimant in social security offices. Far from reducing the frequency of client aggression, however, they are just as likely to increase it by confirming expectations of an impersonal, dehumanised and dehumanising response, and arousing greater frustration at the inaccessibility of the providers. In the language of Mattinson and Sinclair, it is an outward and visible sign that the so-called helpers are, in fact, witholding bastards.

PA found themselves at the opposite end of the spectrum. Under pressure from callers they invariably opted for the 'sucker' position (see especially pp 55 and 57, Chapter 4). On both a personal and an institutional level they avoided setting firm boundaries for fear of being seen, and experiencing themselves as, the withholding bastards. But, as we have seen, this laid them open to all the feelings of exploitation, persecution and being discounted that they were so at pains to avoid engendering in their callers. Nevertheless their implicit assumption that defining boundaries was associated with professional remoteness and unavailability kept them ambivalent for a long time towards doing anything to protect themselves.

Like the Mate and Stalemate clients the PA workers had an image of an idealised, unlimited form of help. They tried to offer this themselves and felt inadequate because they failed to do so. But they also imagined that if they couldn't offer it the professionals could. One worker described these feelings graphically: 'If I manage to get hold of someone I really think is an expert, I feel a lot better about it. If I'm not able to do that, I feel sick.' With this sort of attitude it was no wonder that they found it hard to grasp that the psychiatrist who saw Jenny and the incest abuser described on p 21 were as powerless as they were when confronted by resistance and denial.

Therefore, again like the Mate and Stalemate clients, when the professionals clearly did not live up to their idealised image they were likely to be denigrated as, at best, withholding, unavailable and uninterested and at worst, persecutors—i.e. bastards. One worker who had dealt with the multi-hoax caller wrote to the Director of Social Services to try and get her traced. The Director wrote back to say they had followed up the leads but they had led nowhere and there was nothing further they could do. We thought this an appropriate response but to the worker it was seen as 'dismissive'.

They were particularly suspicious of the police role in incest cases seeing them as insensitive and 'barbaric'. But they also shared the child abuse callers' fears that if they (the callers) made themselves known to social services they would have their children taken away. When a number of callers said that Child Guidance did not understand their difficulties and blamed them for their children's problems this was accepted without question. Unfortunately, their own contacts with professionals did sometimes reinforce these attitudes. Some agencies refused to deal with them when they rang, often in great anxiety, about their callers. A worker who tried to refer to an incest caller was met with a tough investigative response which she felt wheedled out of her more details than she was ready to give and then frightened her by insisting on pursuing the matter further. In short, in these examples the workers were made to feel discounted. They saw PA as existing precisely to counter experiences of this sort. Certainly, this was one of its legitimate functions but it could only be effective if they could find a mid-way position between the suckers and the bastards.

A clue towards a model for such a mid-way position is provided by R D Laing's notion of 'complementarity'. He points out that 'a prototype of the other as giver but not receiver, unresponsive or impervious tends to generate in the self a sense of failure, emptiness and impotence' (Laing 1969). By contrast complementarity is 'that function of personal relations whereby the other fulfils or completes self'. Thus the PA's idealisation of professionals itself resulted in depletion of their sense of their own resources and the apparent imperviousness of professionals to them generated envy and hostility. If, as seems likely, there was a parallel process going on in their callers, an empathic response from a PA worker who did not have to be omnipotent and whose limitations were acknowledged by the existence of appropriate boundaries could provide an important modification for the caller who felt she had nothing to give as a mother and only the 'others', whether PA, professionals or other mothers, somehow had it all. For the depleted caller, prey to envy, a 'sucker' response is as bad as a 'bastard' response since it feeds her greed without allowing her to feel that actually she does have some resources of her own and actually she could end this call and go and attend to her child—and herself.

In fact, some calls were presented where workers *had* been able to set appropriate limits that mediated the either/or polarities of sucker or bastard, persecutor or victim.

> A woman with a 3-year-old daughter, abandoned by her husband, phoned because she was taking out her hurt and frustration on the child. She felt she was a 'useless' mother and was anxious for reassurance that she had not caused 'permament damage' to the child. The worker steered a sensitive course between reassurance which denied the problem and a plea for the child which felt persecuting to the mother. She also encouraged the caller to make clear arrangements with her husband over access, maintenance etc.

Ironically, in the workshop the worker presented her own anxiety that she had *not* given sufficient help or reassurance. The same anxiety was felt by the worker who dealt with the following call in what was, in fact, an excellent model of containment of anxiety.

> A young married woman with an 18-month-old son was alternately crying and silent on the phone. The worker picked up intense anxiety whenever she asked about the child and, after some time of managing to engage the caller in light conversation about child care, asked directly, 'Is your child alright? Have you hurt him?'
>
> The caller confessed that she had but hadn't meant to. She had left him screaming in his cot and he now seemed to have gone to sleep.
>
> The worker praised the caller for leaving the child when it all got too much and suggested she now went to check he was OK, cover him up etc. The caller did so and reported, much to the worker's relief, that the child was OK.
>
> The caller was then able to talk about her own depression and her fear of confronting her husband with her suspicions that he was having an affair.

The worker was left feeling she'd offered nothing!

These two calls show that often the problem was not so much what the workers did as what they felt about it. Clearly the anxieties they were left with were, in part, the result of what had been 'put into them' by the callers. Had they not felt these anxieties they would have been the impervious bastards. Yet neither had they allowed themselves to be overwhelmed—in the first call the worker did not give total reassurance, in the second the worker confronted the abuse directly and thereby rendered the anxieties around it more manageable.

The workers' residual anxieties that they had not given enough reflected an anxiety about limits that was shared by worker and caller alike. If they did not give everything (i.e. became suckers), they had given nothing (i.e. were bastards). The underlying fear was thus of becoming persecutors themselves—exactly the fear that was presented to them by their callers. These basically competent workers needed the workshop to contain their anxieties and give them confidence in the valuable-though-limited job they were doing just as they had struggled to do with their callers. They needed permission to feel what they felt, including, on occasion, anger, frustration and resentment towards callers, without immediately fearing that this made them 'bad'. Idealised images make harsh taskmasters.

In the workshop we were able, by our own contribution, to modify some of the rigid idealisations the workers felt about professionals and this enabled them to take on a more flexible, less persecuting sense of what they should be doing, and to have this sense inform their attitude to callers. After all, if they were afraid to set limits how could they expect the callers to? Most of the callers were worried by precisely the fear that there was no limit to what they might do—a fear that they were both omnipotent and out of control. Yet they were too afraid of the potentially persecuting controls of the statutory services to approach them. PA's very existence as a non-professional agency thus offered a mediation of the extremes of total control versus out of control. Protected by their anonymity callers were able to approach the anonymous parents by a means which remained under their own control. With all this control built in, workers would be playing straight into the callers' omnipotence if they did not set some limits. And, conversely, by setting limits they enabled the callers to accept controls that were not persecuting and might begin to enable them to set non-persecuting limits to their children and themselves.

At the end of the second group of workshops members felt more capable in the work and had greater sense of self-worth and job satisfaction. The workshops had helped them become more self-confident in their status as volunteers by clarifying their aims in a more realistic manner and reminding them that they existed to complement professionals, not to do it all themselves.

We hope that we were also able to convey that, certainly as far as we were concerned, they were highly valued by the professionals they so idealised.

CHAPTER SIX

Parents Anonymous in Context

At the beginning of this study it was stated that it was not our intention to turn PA workers into quasi-professionals. Paradoxically, our success in this respect was related to what has been described as the 'professionalisation' of PA. In other words, the workshops helped them define their task more clearly, increased their competence to perform it and delineated their special area of expertise. All these things made them more professional at what *they* were doing but by the same token enabled them to distinguish themselves from what the professional agencies were doing. Chapter 3 described the particular functions that PA could provide as distinct from professional agencies and Chapter 5 described how, contrary to the workers' implicit fears that it would restrict or even destroy those functions, boundary setting enhanced PA's capacity to perform them.

Nevertheless, there remained considerable anxiety in PA about the value of their role, over and above the particular anxieties aroused in the work. All the workers agreed that in the period immediately preceding and during the workshops (1983-86) the demands made on them had increased not only in quantity but also in quality. There were considerably more 'serious' calls, by which was meant situations involving some kind of desperate emergency and requiring urgent action. There was much speculation as to the reasons for this. Four possible reasons were suggested:

1) The increased profile of PA itself due to media coverage and its change of image portrayed on its poster.
2) An increase in domestic distress due to changes in the social and economic climate—e.g. poverty, unemployment, divorce.
3) An increased public awareness of issues to do with child abuse and incest.
4) Cuts in public service provision.

Obviously these possibilities are not mutually exclusive and indeed there is probably truth in all of them. Although there has been some reduction in unemployment since 1986 it is likely that in the short to medium term all the other factors external to PA are likely to continue to produce increased demands, especially those due to poverty and cuts in public service provision.

Although we helped the PA workers check the omnipotence that made them feel they had to personally solve these problems by soaking up all this increased demand, there remained for them an anxiety that PA was therefore simply a palliative which failed to address their callers' real problems. This anxiety does carry some weight. It is obviously not enough to hide, Pilate-like, behind one's own limitations—the PA workers were right to be concerned about who was going to deal with all those desperate people out there if it was not them. Having thus begun to get a sense of their own role they naturally began to question in a more realistic way where they stood in relation to other agencies, i.e. to see themselves as part of a network which included the professional and statutory services.

These considerations apply not only to PA but more generally to all helplines. The charge of being a palliative is one which might also be levelled at Childline, set up in a blaze of publicity at the end of 1986 amidst rising public concern about child abuse.

In its defence, Childline has always drawn attention to the vast numbers of children who are calling (or attempting to call), suggesting that this shows they are meeting an enormous need. But in fact all the numbers show is that the need is there—it does not say anything about whether the response that Childline makes does anything to alleviate the massive amount of distress and unhappiness that obviously exists in families within our society.

I cannot, of course, speak for Childline of which I have no direct knowledge. However, if PA is anything to go by, the question of whether helplines are palliatives is too global to be answered simply and needs to be broken down in terms of a helpline's various functions before it can be properly addressed.

Of those people that called PA some did not need any further help, some were already in receipt of it and some were too ambivalent to seek it. For all these groups PA provided something additional to anything provided by any other agency and its existence therefore provided for needs which would not otherwise be met. But how far did PA itself meet those needs?

Firstly, it is necessary to distinguish between those needs which can be met and those which can't. This is not something which can be decided in advance but obviously the human lot involves a certain measure of pain and distress and, rather than trying to take it away, a healthy society is one which provides its members with the resources to manage it. The 'listening ear' at times of crisis should not therefore be seen as intended to cure or resolve problems but as a safety valve which enables callers to continue to cope with trying circumstances. It is, however, arguable that such services should properly be available on a statutory basis and in this respect some of the increase in demand for helplines may be due to a shift in the climate of health and welfare provision. Not all the tasks carried out by statutory services are obligatory and in times of rising demand those which are provided on a discretionary basis are the first to go.

In both social services and probation the need to ration resources and justify their use has fostered a climate of managerial efficiency whose emphasis on structured objectives and priorities is inimical to the attitude of openness and availability required for counselling (or what used to be called casework). Counselling is seen as the soft end of social work and while debate rages about the health service, for example, counselling is being quietly privatised without so much as a question in the House. Evidence for this comes from the mushrooming of private counselling and psychotherapy courses and services but it is likely that telephone helplines also pick up a good deal of business from the less motivated and/or those who doubt that counselling would be 'for them' even if they could afford it.

These considerations might lead us to question whether some of those who were already receiving professional help might have had valid complaint when they protested its inadequacy although against this must be reckoned their own ambivalence and idealised expectations of help. Here again is a whole area of need which cannot be met and where the helping process is more about coming to terms with loss and limitation.

As has been previously described, PA was in a uniquely advantageous position to reach those callers who were too ambivalent to seek professional help. In some cases this did lead to callers taking up referrals for professional help (e.g. one worker who had benefited personally from psychotherapy successfully referred a number of callers to psychotherapists, by working with their ambivalence about it over a considerable period of time—all by telephone). But even where this did not happen some useful work could be done via the limited channel along which these ambivalent callers could be reached. This is an extension of the well-known phenomena that many parents will not talk to social workers but are prepared to talk to health visitors.

PA's voluntary status and its independence of the professionals was a great asset here. It does therefore seem appropriate that Childline has followed the lead both of PA and the Samaritans and opted to have trained volunteers rather than professional social workers manning its phones. Like the PA workers these 'ordinary' people are more likely to be able to get alongside the callers and make a direct link with them. Indeed it is questionable whether there is a social work task as such to perform in telephone helpline work. As well as being over-qualified for the job it would create an unhelpful blurring of boundaries.

This brings me to the question of the expectations both callers and the general public have of helplines and it is here that there may be some validity in the 'palliative' charge. In a sense the work so far referred to *is* palliative in that it is limited and not curative. But it does not have the negative connotation of disguising real need or fobbing callers off with an excuse for a proper response. Its role is rather akin to the humanitarian function of the open-door agency for drug addicts I described earlier (p 52). In the case of that project those who favoured a tough rehabilitative approach argued that by providing a palliative we were making it easy for addicts to remain addicts and actually preventing them seeking rehabilitation. Our counter-argument was that to take the extreme case, some addicts would rather die than seek rehabilitation and we had a duty to help them as best we could. This did not, however, prevent us from excluding those who abused the centre's facilities.

Likewise, there is little or nothing to be said for refusing to offer help to those who insist on remaining anonymous, even though they may be putting their children at risk. If PA was not available they would not be likely to seek help at all. But, as with the drug project, there are those callers who abuse the facilities of anonymity, particularly the incest callers and in the course of the workshops the workers learnt how to show them the metaphorical door.

To follow the analogy of the drug project one step further: it is true that we tended to overestimate our therapeutic function for the addicts but by no stretch of the imagination could we be said to be rehabilitating them. Had we attempted to present ourselves as a rehabilitative project our critics would have been more than justified in their strictures.

It is thus dangerous and misleading for helplines to present themselves as capable of doing what they are not. At best this might salve the public conscience by making it appear that 'something is being done'; at worst it might encourage the belief that they are capable of dealing with their callers' problems. This way of putting it points up the fine line helplines have to tread. Obviously, in promoting themselves helplines have to inspire hope and confidence—this is their proper function and people are hardly likely to call if they cannot expect to be helped. But if their usefulness is promoted to excess they can only raise expectations that cannot be fulfilled. The proper role of helplines is to be a pointer towards help or, more generally, a confirmation that help is a possibility. The attempt to offer anything more substantive is vitiated by the inbuilt limits of telephone communication.

This may well explain why Childline has come in for so much criticism—its high public profile, though in one sense necessary for its success, is at odds with its actual function. In this respect it is an exception amongst helplines in having been launched from the 'top down' as a large scale organisation. Most helplines arise as a result of grass roots initiative and only gradually assume any substantial public profile. I would argue that, while not essential, being seen as unassuming and small-scale is an advantage in matching callers' expectations with the reality of what is likely to be provided. The impact of media attention on PA was certainly difficult for it to manage. Misled by media publicity some callers seemed to view the workers as omnipotent founts of authority—a further variation on a familiar theme.

Demands of this sort make it all the more necessary that helplines are able to make connections with adequate back-up services. It is ironic that while, on the one hand, Childline is engaged in the search for massive funds to expand its operations, its director has expressed serious concern about the crisis prevailing in London's social services departments which cannot cope with current demands let alone the increased demand aroused, in part, by the high publicity profile of Childline (*New Society*, 20 November 1987). This is not to deny the value and importance of Childline in mitigating the despair of abused children but to underline the need for professionals and volunteers to work together as part of an overall network. Helplines exist to fill a gap in statutory provision and provide a *necessary* palliative where deeper remedies are not possible but the more resources are channelled only toward *them* rather than those who might do more palliate, the greater the gap becomes and the less helplines can be expected to fill it.

The bitter reality is that most callers to helplines will have to struggle on as best they can with the difficulties that beset them. As should by now be clear, this applies regardless of the quality of statutory provision though this is, of course, much more the case where statutory provision is lacking. No helpline is ever going to eradicate child abuse any more than the Samaritans are going to stop people wanting to commit suicide. But it does make a difference whether one is struggling on with hope or without it. This is at its most explicit for the Samaritans where the choice is whether or not to struggle on at all. Their success in bringing people back from the brink underlines most starkly the power of the hope which is evoked by there being *someone* who can hear and will listen and will try to understand. That is better, sometimes a lot better, than nothing. And, even more, hope can sometimes act as a catalyst, helping callers reach out for help elsewhere—if and when it is available.

If helplines are able to provide this kind of service, and in our work with PA we saw plenty of evidence that they do, then they have an important role to play in our society and their difficult work will not be in vain.

Postscript

In October 1988 Evelyn Cleavely and I met once more with the members of Parents Anonymous who had attended the workshops to hear their reactions to the draft of the monograph. They felt that it was a fair and helpful account of their work but also told us that the organisation had moved on in the intervening two years, partly as a result of the workshops themselves. In order to bring the record up to date I include here a brief summary of those developments.

Although they still felt dogged by feelings of helplessness and inadequacy there is now more recognition that this is what they get left with by callers and there is more support available in the organisation to deal with such feelings. The support groups, for example, are more structured and work more effectively with emotional issues, new workers are paired with experienced ones to make it easier for them to seek and receive support, and there is a constructive awareness of where the support network still needs to be improved.

They confirmed the impact of the workshops outlined in Chapter 5—that they had given them permission to value themselves, not to feel they had to be omnipotent and to recognise the value of setting limits. Generally, their sense of self-esteem and confidence seemed to have risen considerably.

The organisation as a whole has become more structured although they said it was incredible how much is still done with so little organisation. The workshops had crystallised the need for a change of direction in Parents Anonymous and it is now accepted that they should be a listening agency rather than an information-giving one. Training is now longer and focused on the development of a capacity to listen. There is also more ongoing training. One worker—the one who barraged the mother of the tantrum toddler with practical information (p 39)—reported that she had not needed to use her information pack for two years.

References

Bannister, K and Pincus, L (1965) *Shared Phantasy in Marital Problems*, Tavistock Institute of Marital Studies

Butler-Sloss, E (1988) *Report of the Inquiry into Child Abuse in Cleveland 1987*, HMSO

Curry, D (1984) The Wounding Healer—Pathology of a Profession, unpublished

De La Noy, M (1987) *Acting as Friends. The Story of the Samaritans*, Constable

Dylan, B (1965) It's all right Ma, I'm only bleeding. On *Bringing it all Back Home*, CBS Records

Eco, U (1984) *The Name of the Rose*, Paladin

Groesbeck, C J (1975) The Archetypal Image of the Wounded Healer, *Jnl. of Analytical Psychology* 20, pp 123–45

Haug, M and Susman, M B (1969/70) Professional Autonomy and the Revolt of the Client, *Social Problems* Vol 17, No. 2

Jacques, E (1955) Social Systems as a defence against persecutory and depressive anxiety. In *New Directions in Psychoanalysis*, Tavistock

Jung, C G (1912/1952) Symbols of Transformation. In *Collected Works* Vol 5, Routledge and Kegan Paul

Jung, C G (1931) Problems of Modern Psychotherapy. In *Collected Works*, Vol 16, Routledge and Kegan Paul

Karpman, S (1968) Fairy Tales and Script Drama Analysis. *Transactional Analysis Bulletin* Vol 7, pp 39–43

Laing, R D (1969) *Self and Others*, Tavistock

Marshall, T (1963) *Sociology at the Crossroads*, Heinemann

Masson, J (1984) *Freud: The Assault on Truth*, Faber and Faber

Mattinson, J (1975) *The Reflection Process in Casework Supervision*, Tavistock Institute of Marital Studies

Mattinson, J and Sinclair, I (1979) *Mate and Stalemate*, Basil Blackwell

Menzies, I E P (1959) The Functions of Social Systems as a Defence Against Anxiety: in *Containing Anxiety in Institutions: Selected Essays Vol. 1* pp 43–85, Free Association Books

Sartre, J P (1969) *Being and Nothingness* (trans Hazel Barnes)

Varah, C (1973) *The Samaritans in the '70s*, Constable

Wilding, P (1982) *Professional Power and Social Welfare*, Routledge and Kegan Paul

Winnicott, D W (1971) *Playing and Reality*, Penguin